Joseph Warren Keifer

Official Reports of J. Warren Keifer

Brevet Major General of Volunteers, U. S. A., Detailing Movements and

Operations of his Command in the Battles of Winchester (1863)...

Joseph Warren Keifer

Official Reports of J. Warren Keifer
Brevet Major General of Volunteers, U. S. A., Detailing Movements and Operations of his Command in the Battles of Winchester (1863)...

ISBN/EAN: 9783744740968

Printed in Europe, USA, Canada, Australia, Japan

Cover: Foto ©ninafisch / pixelio.de

More available books at **www.hansebooks.com**

OFFICIAL REPORTS

—OF—

J. WARREN KEIFER,

BREVET MAJOR GENERAL OF VOLUNTEERS,

U. S. A.

WHILE SERVING IN THE ARMIES

OF THE

POTOMAC AND SHENANDOAH.

●◆●

CONTENTS: PAGES:

SPRINGFIELD:
DAILY REPUBLIC STEAM JOB ROOMS.

1866.

OFFICIAL REPORTS

OF

J. WARREN KEIFER,

Brevet Major General of Volunteers,

.

U. S. A.

Detailing movements and operations of his command in the battles of Winches-
ter (1863); Brandy Station, Orange Grove, Wilderness, Spotsylvania,
Cold Harbor, Petersburg (1864): Monocacy, Opequon, Fisher's
Hill, Cedar Creek, Petersburg (1865), and Sailor's
Creek, also, prior to and at the surrender
of General Lee's Army.

———————— •◦► ◄◦• ——— --

SPRINGFIELD, OHIO:
DAILY REPUBLIC STEAM JOB OFFICE.
::::::::::::::::
1866.

Dedication.

TO BREVET BRIGADIER GENERALS
Wm. H. Ball, John W. Horn, M. R. McClennan.

COLONEL
B. F. Smith,

BREVET COLONELS
Otho H. Binkley, Moses M. Granger, James W. Snyder.

LIEUTENANT COLONELS
W. N. Foster, T. M. McKinney, J. C. Hill,

BREVET LIEUTENANT COLONELS
Aaron Spangler, S. B. Lamareaux, Anson Wood, Wm. Wood,

BREVET MAJORS
Luther Brown, G. W. Brinkerhoff, Henry J. Rhodes, Chauncey Fish and the brave officers and men, who served under them;

Also, BREVET MAJORS
Jonathan T. Rorer, Wm. L. Shaw, T. J. Hoskinson, J. F. Hazelton, J. P. Dudrow,

CAPTAINS
Thomas Black, Harrison D'Yarmett and the other members of my Staff; and also,

TO THE MEMORY OF
Lieutenant Colonel Aaron W. Ebright,
Brevet Colonel Clifton K. Prentiss,
Major Wm. S. McElwain,
Captains Wm. A. Hathaway, Thomas J. Hyatt, Wm. H. Burns, Orson Howard, Thomas Kilburn, Wesley Devenny, Wm. R. Moore, Joshua Deter, Henry H. Stevens, and
the many other brave officers and
men, their comrades in battle,
who yielded up their
lives in defense
of their
country,

These reports are most *respectfully and affectionately inscribed*

BY THE AUTHOR,
Who ever appreciated them for their gallantry, zeal and patriotism, in camp, on the toilsome march and upon the field of mortal combat. So long as brave, earnest and self-sacrificing officers and men of the Union Army, are held in grateful remembrance by patriotic people and true lovers of human liberty, it is believed that the name of these officers and men will be honored and respected.

Preface.

The official reports published in this volume detail the principal movements and operations of the 2nd Brigade, 3rd Division, 3rd Army Corps, in the year 1863, and of the same Brigade in the 3rd Division, 6th Army Corps, in the years 1864 and 1865, in the Army of the Potomac, including those of the 3rd Division, 6th Army Corps at the memorable battle of Cedar Creek, Va., October, 1864, under Maj. Genl.'s Wright and Sheridan, and also, including the part taken by the 110th Ohio Volunteer Infantry at Winchester, June, 1863.

They are printed from exact copies of official reports, written, as required by orders from Army, Corps and Division Head Quarters.

In consequence of very proper orders issued by the War Department, no official reports were allowed to be published during the War, save by permission of the "proper authority."

The officers and soldiers who participated in the movements and battles of the War deserve to have their services laid before the public, by the publication of the official reports.

These reports are published for gratuitous circulation among the officers and soldiers of the command to which they refer, with the hope that they may be appreciated by them.

All that is contained in this volume, aside from official reports, was written with a view to show the movements of troops in the intervals of time between the important operations recited in the reports.

Nominal and summary lists of casualties are omitted after each report, but a general summary by Regiments, of casualties in the several engagements, is appended.

Springfield, Ohio.

Battles of Winchester, June 1863.

HEADQUARTERS, 110TH OHIO VOL. INFANTRY,
1ST BRIG., 2D DIVISION, 8TH ARMY CORPS,
Harper's Ferry, Va., June 16th, 1863.

CAPTAIN—*Dear Sir:* In compliance with an order from Brig. Gen. W. L. Elliott, I have to report the following operations of my command on the 13th, 14th and 15th days of June, 1863:

On the morning of the 13th inst. I was ordered with my Regiment to march upon the Cedar Creek road. Arriving at Union Mills, on the Strasburg road, it was ascertained that the enemy were in force upon that road, at or near Kearnstown: About 10 A. M., under the direction of General Elliott, I marched my Regiment to the right of the Strasburg road accompanied by one Section of Carlin's Battery, commanded by Lieutenant Theaker. The Infantry did not become engaged and were withdrawn about 1 P. M. to the mouth of the Cedar Creek road.

At 2 P. M. I received an order to take my Regiment, the 12th Pennsylvania Volunteer Cavalry, commanded by Lieutenant Colonel Moss and the Section of Carlin's Battery, commanded by Lieutenant Theaker, and make a reconnoisance.

I moved at once, up the Strasburg road, forming my Infantry upon the right and center, Artillery in center and Cavalry upon the left. The Infantry on the right was commanded by Lieutenant Colonel Foster, and in the center by Major Binkley. After proceeding about one mile the Infantry and Cavalry skirmishers became closely engaged with the enemy's advance.

The enemy were driven back to a woods upon the left. I immediately withdrew the Cavalry skirmishers, who were beginning to suffer severely from the enemy's sharp shooters, placed the Artillery in position and shelled the woods, where the enemy were concealed in large force. After a few minutes brisk firing the enemy fell back to a woods upon the left of Kearnstown. I advanced with the entire force under a heavy Infantry fire to within one-fourth of a mile of the town, and opened upon the enemy with canister, producing a telling effect: at the same time the Infantry on my right became closely engaged. In ten minutes the enemy retreated beyond the town, having suffered severely.

My flankers from the right reported the enemy turning my right flank, with at least one Brigade of Infantry. I withdrew the command in perfect order, keeping my skirmishers well to the front, embracing every opportunity the ground afforded to halt, and with Artillery, to pour a heavy fire into the enemy's ranks. At Union Mills, after a spirited engagement, the enemy were repulsed with heavy loss. General Elliott, having come up with reinforcements, I brought off all my killed and wounded. Lieutenant Theaker deserves great praise for the skill exhibited in handling his guns, while under my command.

Except some skirmishing with the enemy's sharpshooters, this ended the operations of my command on the 13th. Being relieved by the 122d Ohio Volunteer Infantry, I withdrew my Regiment to its camp on the heights of Winchester about 10 P. M. On the 14th inst. I was ordered by General Elliott to occupy the earthwork between the Pughtown and Romney roads, which was an isolated earthwork of slight strength about ¾ of a mile from the main fort, and fully commanded by Round Mountain on the west. I took position at 7. A. M. The works were also occupied by one company of the 116th Ohio Volunteer Infantry, commanded by Captain Arckenoe, and Company "L," 5th U. S. Artillery, commanded by Lieutenant Randolph. We remained unmolested until about 5 P. M., when the enemy having placed at least sixteen pieces of heavy Artillery in position, on Round Mountain, opened a heavy cannonade upon us. Battery "L" replied until about 50 Artillery horses were killed and the caissons and the limber carriages were blown up, and knocked to pieces. Two guns only could be kept in position to await the approach of an assaulting party of the enemy. About 6 P. M. the enemy came up behind a ridge to our front, with at least five Regiments in deep column of attack, the advance Regiment carrying the United States colors. The enemy was able to come up under cover, to within one hundred yards of the works. The Infantry and Artillery opened fire upon him with fearful effect, mowing down his advance Regiment almost to a man. My sharpshooters shot down the officers on horseback, but only for a few moments could we check the enemy's advancing column, and with terrible loss he effected an entrance into the works near the center of my Regiment, my men fighting him until he outnumbered us inside the works. The trenches and breastworks were of such a character as to afford no obstructions to the entrance of the enemy.*

I withdrew my command under cover of the guns at the main fort, with a loss of forty killed, wounded and captured in my own Regiment. The whole number of killed and wounded was very small.

The guns of the Battery were lost. I would do injustice to Lieutenant Randolph and his officers if I did not make favorable mention of their conduct. Lieutenant Randolph had three horses shot under him while in the works.

From the commanding position of the enemy's guns and their superiority in number and weight, it was impossible to effectively reply to them.

The enemy's loss in their attack did not fall short of four hundred men in killed and wounded. It may have exceeded that number largely. Lieutenant Paris Horney, of the 110th Ohio Regiment, was captured or killed, while fighting the enemy at the works. Captain Arckenoe, 116th Ohio Volunteer Infantry, was killed while nobly urging on his men, his face to the foe.

*The following is an extract from the official report of Major General R. H. Milroy: "The enemy opened upon me with at least four full Batteries, some of his guns being of the longest range, under cover of which fire, he precipitated a column at least *ten thousand* strong upon the out work held by Colonel Keifer, which, after a stubborn resistance he carried."

My regiment remained under a heavy Artillery fire in the outer works of the main fort until dark, with little or no loss.

At 2 A. M. on the 15th inst., after abandoning all the sick, wounded and baggage, under orders from the commanding General, the Regiment was marched out from the main works, numbering nineteen officers and less than four hundred men, with the understanding that the entire command was to cut through the enemy's lines to Harper's Ferry. Company " D." of my Regiment, commanded by Captain McElwaln, was detached from the Regiment on Saturday night; also Lieutenants Weakley and Gross. with sixty men of the Regiment, were sent on picket on the morning of the 13th. I have learned nothing definite of their fate since, but have strong hopes that most if not all escaped on the 15th inst.

Lieutenants Cron and Miller were left sick. Lieutenant Cron fought bravely with his men on the 13th and 14th. Assistant Surgeon R. R. McCandliss and Chaplain James Harvey, of my Regiment, were ordered by me to remain with the sick and wounded.

After marching about four miles from Winchester, on the Martinsburg road, firing commenced upon our front and right. My Regiment formed in line of battle under orders from General Elliott. Skirmishers were thrown forward, and the line advanced for a short distance to the north-ward. My Regiment was on the left of the 123d Ohio Regiment, and on the extreme left.

By direction of General Elliott I moved my command by the left flank to the northward on a line parallel with the Martinsburg road until my left was about five miles from Winchester. The enemy opened fire upon the 123d Ohio with Artillery and Infantry, from a woods immediately on the east side of the Martinsburg road. I formed my line facing the east, where the enemy was discovered in my front, in the woods and behind stone walls. (Prisoners, afterward captured, claimed to belong to the notorious Stonewall Brigade, now commanded by General Walker.)

With the consent of General Elliott I charged the enemy with my Regiment: outflanking him upon his right, driving him through the woods upon his Artillery, occupying the woods on the east of the road, opening a destructive fire into his ranks, throwing him into confusion and killing and wounding large numbers. We also silenced the enemy's guns (twelve pounders) immediately in our front, capturing one of his caissons. In a few minutes the woods were cleared. Not being supported upon my right the enemy soon appeared in large numbers in that direction, with two heavy pieces of Artillery. I withdrew my Regiment a short distance, changed direction to the right and again advanced on the enemy.

The 122d Ohio Volunteer Infantry (Colonel Ball) came up to my support on the right and in twenty minutes we once more cleared the woods in our front, shooting down gunners and horses of the enemy's Artillery and bringing off some of his horses; we were only deterred from taking possession of the guns, by a large body of the enemy again appearing on our right.

Without waiting the enemy's fire I ordered both Regiments to withdraw, which was effected in good order to the west of the Martinsburg road. The enemy re-occupied the woods in superior force. Again I ordered a charge into the woods which was nobly responded to by both officers and men. After a severe conflict, in which the two lines were engaged as near in places as 20 feet, pouring a murderous fire into each other's breasts, the enemy gave way and our line advanced upon the enemy's Artillery, shooting or driving his gunners away from their pieces and completely silencing them. My whole line was then, by my order, withdrawn from the woods, and under the direction of the General commanding, marched to Harper's Ferry, arriving at that place at 2 P. M., having marched a distance of 35 miles and fighting two hours on the way.

I brought with me eighteen officers and three hundred and five men. Captain E. A. Shephard fell from weakness and exhaustion, possibly wounded while cheering on his men, and was carried from the field, but was afterwards captured. Judging from the dead and wounded of the enemy I saw upon the field, from the relative positions occupied, and the steady, close fire of my men. I estimate the enemy's loss at more than three hundred men immediately in my front, on the morning of the 15th instant.

My own loss in killed and wounded was about seventy, few of the number killed, many slightly wounded.

During the series of engagements of the three days, my officers and men performed valiant service. It is no less a pleasure than a duty to commend them all for skill, coolness and bravery. I think proper to make special mention of the fact, that each officer remained with his own command, doing his duty and urging on his men by his example. To this fact I attribute my success in keeping my men together. I cannot close this report without making special mention of Lieutenant-Colnel W. N. Foster and Major O. II. Binkley. They were not only fearless of danger, but showed superior skill in each separate engagement. They were always present where danger was greatest, or where their duty called them. Adjutant J. B. Van Eaton was present always in the thickest of the fight, gallantly discharging his duty. It would be but simple justice to say the same of Captains Smith. Moore, Spangler, Ullery, Snodgrass, and Brown; Lieutenants Hathaway, Rush, Cannon, Shellabarger, McKnight, Moore, and Boyer; also, Sergeant Traub. The latter commanded a detachment of Company "K" through each engagement. Captain Snodgrass received two wounds, but did not leave the field.

Running further risk of being censured for making special mention of men, where all behaved so nobly, I cannot refrain from calling attention to my sharpshooters, armed with the Henry rifle. In each engagement, they poured an almost continual stream of fire into the enemy's ranks, causing a great loss of life. They also, under my own observation, shot down a number of the enemy's officers.

The total number of my killed, wounded, missing in action, and left in camp and hospital, was three hundred and fifteen, including two commissioned staff officers and four line officers.

This estimate does not include Company " D " and its officers, Lieutenants Weakly and Gross, Assistant Surgeon Owen and Q. M. Stark, supposed to have escaped on the 15th inst. Captain McElwain and his company distinguished themselves by the splendid manner in which they engaged the enemy's sharpshooters and drove them from the woods, on the evening of the 13th. Lieutenants Weakly, Gross and Trimble fought bravely with their men on the 13th and 14th. The vastly superior force of the enemy, and the many other discouraging circumstances under which he was engaged, the splendid manner in which my command confronted him, and the energy and skill exhibited in getting the greater portion of the effective strength through his strong lines, furnish high proof of the soldierly character and efficiency of the troops.

Hoping you will pardon the length of this necessarily unsatisfactory and incomplete report, I remain very truly, Captain, your most obedient and humble servant,

J. WARREN KEIFER,
Colonel 110th Ohio Vol. Inf., Comd'g.

J. ELLIOTT JACOBS,
Captain and A. A. G., 1st Brig. 2d Div. 8th A. C.

———

CAMP AT BRANDY STATION, December 22d, 1863.

I have the honor to submit the following supplemental report of the operations of the 110th Ohio Volunteer Infantry on the 13th, 14th and 15th days of June, 1863:

The official report, to which this is a supplement, dated June 16th, 1863, was written from the best data that could then be procured. The movements of the regiment are accurately stated in the original report.

The losses in killed and wounded have since been ascertained to be light in a remarkable degree, compared with the losses of the enemy.— Information of a reliable character received from citizens of Winchester Va., also from published accounts of the enemy, and from admissions made by officers and soldiers captured from him, who were engaged in the contests of the three days at and near Winchester, make it safe to estimate his loss in the assault upon our works, on the evening of the 14th of June, 1863, at one hundred killed and four hundred wounded.— Some reports fix the loss at over two hundred killed, besides a large number wounded. The loss of the enemy in the attack made by the regiment, on the morning of the 15th of June, 1863, exceeded two hundred killed and a proportionate number wounded.

The total loss of the 110th Ohio Volunteer Infantry, in the operations of the three days, not including the captured, was four (4) enlisted men killed, and one officer and fifty enlisted men wounded.

The great disparity in losses is owing to the fact that, on the 14th, the regiment was protected by earthworks, while the enemy exposed himself to a heavy fire of Infantry and artillery while charging in column.— Also, on the morning of the 15th, the enemy was attacked, surprised and for a considerable time, by the rapid firing of the men, kept in disorder. It is also partly attributable to the further fact, that when the enemy succeeded in forming to repel the attack, my troops were each time withdrawn before receiving his fire, and a new direction taken, which enabled me to attack the enemy upon his flank and rear, thereby compelling him to fall back, suffering each time heavy loss.

The artillery, attempted to be used by the enemy on the 15th, was not effective, and was soon silenced by the well-directed infantry fire poured upon it.

It is worthy of note that the proportion of killed to the wounded in the regiment, was little more than seven per cent.

Lieutenant Cron, reported captured, escaped with Captain McElwain's company into Pennsylvania. Lieutenant Weakley was left with sixty men upon picket, in consequence of his whereabouts not being known to me, and a false report that he was with the wagon train.

The Lieutenant, with most of the men, were left at their posts on picket, and alone engaged the enemy at Winchester on the morning of the 15th. They, after a most gallant resistance, surrendered.

The total number captured was five officers, and two hundred and forty-three enlisted men, including the sick and thirty-eight of the wounded. A part of the sick and wounded were recaptured in July following.

One officer and twelve enlisted men, slightly wounded, escaped with the regiment.

Assistant-Surgeon Thomas C. Owen was captured on the field, June 15th, but escaped from the enemy at Martinsburg in July following.

A list of the captured officers, and the killed and wounded officers and enlisted men, is hereto appended.

I am very respectfully your obedient and humble servant,

J. WARREN KEIFER,
Colonel Commanding.

The 110th and 122d Ohio, 6th Maryland, and 138th Pennsylvania Infantry Regiments, were organized into the 2d Brigade, 2d Division, 8th A. C., on the 16th day of June, 1863, at Harper's Ferry, Va., which, as a brigade organization, was not broken up until after the close of the war.

The brigade participated in the evacuation of Maryland Heights, and, with other troops, guarded the heavy guns, ammunition, and other government property, on canal boats to Washington City, arriving at that place July 4th.

On the 6th of July, it shipped by rail to Fredericksburg, Md., and on the 9th of July arrived, joined and became the 2d Brigade, 3d Division, 3d Army Corps, Army of the Potomac, and immediately engaged in the pursuit of the rebel army of Northern Virginia, which was then retreating from the fatal field of Gettysburg.

On the night of July 13th, the enemy escaped across the Potomac River at Williamsport and Falling Waters, and was rapidly pursued by the Army of the Potomac into Virginia, by the way of Harper's Ferry.

The enemy retreated up the valley to Front Royal. The Army of the Potomac continued the pursuit, keeping along the east side of the Blue

Ridge, passing through Upperville and Piedmont to Manassas Gap, where, on the 23d of July, a very brisk skirmish took place, in which the brigade came under fire.

On the 26th, the army arrived at Warrenton, the rebel army having taken up a position behind the Rapidan, covering Raccoon and other fords. About the 6th of August, the brigade went into camp near Foxes' Ford, on the Rappahannock River.

On the 15th, the two Ohio regiments started to New York City to aid in enforcing the draft, at which place they arrived on the 21st, going by rail and steamship. While at New York, the 110th Ohio was in camp on Governor's Island and in Carroll Park, Brooklyn.

On the 6th of September, the Ohio troops reshipped for Alexandria, from thence marched, and on the 14th rejoined the brigade at the place they had left it.

On the 15th, the army moved across the Rappahannock to Culpepper Court House. The brigade went into camp two miles from Culpepper, on the Sperryville Road, where it remained until October 10th, 1863.

HEADQUARTERS 2D BRIGADE, 3D DIVISION, 3D A. C.
CAMP NEAR BEALTON STATION, VA.,
November 3, 1863.

LIEUT.—*Sir:* In compliance with circular from Division Headquarters, I have the honor to report the following movements and operations of my command, (composed of the 110th and 122d Ohio, 6th Md., and 138th Penn. Volunteer Infantry Regiments,) from the commencement of the march from Culpepper C. H. to the present time:

On the 10th of October, 1863, my camp, (located two miles from Culpepper C. H., on the Sperryville Road,) was broken up in pursuance of an order from Brigadier-General Carr, commanding 3d. Div. 3d A. C., and the troops in my command took up a position a short distance to the front of my camp, to meet an attack of the enemy, should one be made. On the morning of the 11th we left our position and marched to the rear, and crossed the Rappahannock River about 11 P. M., at Freeman's Ford. On the evening of the 12th, the 138th Pennsylvania Volunteer Infantry was detailed as train guard to the corps ammunition and ambulance trains, and did not rejoin the brigade until the 22d.

On the 13th my brigade was ordered to take the advance of the corps, and march upon the road leading to "Three Mile Station," on the Warrenton Branch Railroad. Captain Winslow's Battery, 1st New York Artillery, reported to me, and was with my brigade on its march to "Three Mile Station." Flankers were thrown out, as well as an advance guard kept well to the front. My brigade arrived at "Three Mile Station" without incident, about 12 P. M. (During a temporary halt at this place the Ohio troops voted.) About 3 P. M. the brigade moved in the advance of the division for Greenwich, arriving at that place about 9 P.M. The head of the column of the 1st Division was engaged near Auburn. My brigade was ordered forward to take part, but arrived after the enemy was retreating. During this day's march my brigade was under the immediate direction of, and was accompanied by, Brigadier-General Carr.

On the 14th inst., I was, with my brigade, ordered to form the rear guard of the 3d Corps. Captain McKnight's 12th New York Battery reported to me to accompany the rear guard. I received verbal instructions from Brigadier-General Carr to cover the rear with a good rear guard, avoid bringing on a general engagement, and as far as possible baffle the enemy in his endeavors to delay the main column. The corps arrived at Bristoe Station about 12 M. The enemy, with a small force of cavalry and a large body of infantry, followed closely, but did not attack. He succeeded in capturing few if any stragglers from the 3d Corps.

After a short halt at Bristoe Station, the 3d Corps moved by the way of Manassas Heights toward Centerville. At Manassas Heights I received an order from a staff officer of the General Commanding, to take position and hold the Heights of Manassas until the arrival of the 5th A. C.— Brigadier-General W. H. Morris, commanding 1st Brigade, also took position upon the heights at Manassas. Upon the arrival of the 5th A. C., I marched my brigade across Bull Run at Blackman's Ford. Under the direction of the Brigadier-General Commanding Division, I took up a position with my command for the night, covering, with the other troops of the 3d Division, Mitchell's Ford.

On the 14th the troops marched to Union Mills, via Centerville. The troops remained at Union Mills until October 19th, when they marched to near Bristoe Station.

On the 20th, marched again to near Greenwich. On the 21st day of October, marched to Catlett's Station. My brigade remained at the latter-named place until the 23d, when, in compliance with an order emanating from Corps Headquarters, marched to Bristoe Station and relieved Brigadier-General Merritt's cavalry command, stationed at that place. My brigade was relieved at Bristoe Station by the 1st A. C., Oct. 24th, and in accordance with orders from Division Headquarters, rejoined the division at Catlett's Station, October 25th, '63. The brigade changed position, under the direction of the division commander, about 9 P. M. to cover the ford over Cedar Run, near Weaversville. On the 26th, about 9 P. M., the brigade again changed position, and formed line of battle with the left resting on the railroad, about 1½ miles north of Catlett's Station.

At 3 P. M. October 28th, I received orders from Division Headquarters to proceed with my brigade to near Bealton Station, and relieve the 3d Brigade, 3d Division, (Colonel Smith's.) I marched the same evening, relieved Colonel Smith's Brigade, and encamped on the right of the railroad, about two miles from Bealton Station, which position the brigade still occupies.

During the time included in this report, nothing of any special importance occurred in the operations of my brigade. My orders were, with one exception, received from, or through, the Division Commander; in many instances on the march, from the Division Commander in person.

Considering the amount of rations (eight days') constantly required to be kept on the person of the soldier, and the loss of sleep occasioned by night marching, the troops in my command endured the march very well. Eight men are yet absent and unaccounted for, who straggled upon the march. From the best information, it is thought that they were not captured, but wilfully separated themselves from the command, and escaped to the rear. The officers were, with few exceptions, prompt in the discharge of their duties; and especially was this the case upon the part of regimental commanders.

All were separated, during the march to the rear, from their baggage, and suffered uncomplainingly the many consequent inconveniences and privations.

Lieutenants Hathaway, Yarger and Black, members of my staff, rendered all possible assistance on the march in keeping the command together, keeping up stragglers from other commands, as well as my own, and in carrying out orders generally.

I am, Lieutenant, very respectfully, your obedient and humble servant,

J. WARREN KEIFER,

Colonel Commanding.

J. Johnson, 1st Lieut. and A. A. A. G., 3d Div., 3d A. C.

Battle of Brandy Station.

HEADQUARTERS 2D BRIGADE, 3D DIVISION, 3D A. C.,
CAMP AT BRANDY STATION, VA.,
November 10th, 1863.

LIEUTENANT—Sir: I have the honor to report, in compliance with Circular Order of this date from Headquarters 3d Division, 3d A. C., the following movements and operations of my command since leaving our camp, four miles south of Warrenton Junction, Va. My brigade is composed of the 6th Md., 138th Penn., 122d and 110th Ohio Infantry Regiments, commanded respectively by Colonels John W. Horn, M. R. McClennan, Wm. H. Ball, and Lieutenant-Colonel W. N. Foster.

On the night of the 6th inst., at 11½ o'clock, I received a written order from Division Headquarters to report with my brigade at Division Headquarters at daylight on the 7th inst., in readiness to march, the men to have eight days' rations on their persons. I reported in accordance with the order.

At 8 A. M., my brigade moved in the rear of the 1st Brigade of the 3d Division, toward Kelly's Ford, over the Rappahannock River, arriving at that place at about 1 P. M. The brigade was massed near a brick church, about ⅓ of a mile from Kelly's Ford, as directed by a verbal order from Division Headquarters. About 2½ P. M., we changed position to the heights to the left of the Ford, as directed by a similar order from Division Headquarters. I received orders from Division Headquarters to cross the Rappahannock about 5 P. M. After some temporary delay at the pontoon bridge, I crossed the river, and bivouaced the troops in line of battle, by battalions in mass, in the rear of the 3d Brigade, facing in a southerly direction. The brigade was put in position under the direction of General Carr, Commanding 3d Division. Two hundred men were detailed by me from the 6th Maryland Infantry, under the command of Major J. C. Hill, of the same regiment, for picket duty, as directed by verbal orders from Division Headquarters. I personally assisted in posting the pickets in front of the 3d Division, 3d Corps, causing them to connect with pickets of the 1st and 2d Divisions of the 3d Corps on the right and left.

A circular order was received from Division Headquarters to have the men under arms at daylight, and in readiness to march.

At 4 A. M., November 8th, a verbal order was received to detail two regiments immediately to make a reconnoissance to the front. Accordingly the 122d and 110th Ohio Infantry were detailed, and under the command of Colonel Wm. H. Ball, 122d Ohio Infantry, proceeded to make the reconnoissance, taking with them one company of the 6th Maryland Infantry that had been on picket. The reconnoissance advanced about 1½ miles, discovering the enemy in no force. At the late camp of the enemy, three officers and thirty-five enlisted men were captured. My brigade was then ordered to take the advance of the division and corps, which was the advance of the army. The march was resumed in the direction of Brandy Station, Va., 6th Maryland Infantry in the advance of the brigade.

About 2½ miles from Brandy Station, and on the line of the Orange & Alexandria Railroad, the advance encountered the rebels in considerable force, principally cavalry with horse artillery. After a short halt, my command was disposed in order of battle to advance and drive the enemy from a hill which he occupied in some force, with artillery in position. The brigade was formed with the 6th Maryland Infantry upon the right, 110th Ohio Infantry upon the right of the railroad and in the center, the 138th Pennsylvania Infantry upon the left, supported by the 122d Ohio Infantry. Upon the right of the railroad, in front of the 110th Ohio and 6th Maryland Infantry Regiments, skirmishers were advanced from each regiment.

The 138th Pennsylvania Volunteer Infantry was ordered to deploy to the left of the railroad as soon as an advance was ordered. The 122d Ohio was ordered to closely support the 138th Pennsylvania.

An order was received from Division Headquarters to advance two companies as skirmishers, one upon each side of the railroad. One company from the 110th Ohio, commanded by Lieutenant Fox, and one company from the 138th Pennsylvania, commanded by Captain Fisher, were advanced. An order was received from Division Headquarters to move forward two regiments of my brigade. Accordingly, the 110th Ohio and 138th Pennsylvania V. I., were ordered forward. The 138th Pennsylvania soon came under the enemy's artillery fire. The skirmishers were rapidly pushed forward, supported by the two regiments named, and the hill was soon carried. Captain Lazarus C. Andress, 138th Pennsylvania Volunteer Infantry, fell mortally wounded. Orderly Sergeant A. G. Rapp, Co. "H," 138th P. V. I., lost his left arm, and was otherwise slightly wounded. Five other members of this regiment received slight but not dangerous wounds.

As soon as the hill was gained, I ordered the skirmishers and the two regiments that were in the advance, to pursue the enemy.

The pursuit was continued, with constant skirmishing, until the enemy was driven past Brandy Station, at which place the troops were ordered to halt by an order from Brigadier-General Carr. The enemy placed artillery in position and shelled my brigade, wounding two men slightly in the 122d Ohio Infantry. The brigade bivouaced near Brandy Station until this morning, when orders were received for it to go into camp at the Station, in which position it still remains.

Officers and men were prompt in obeying orders. The manner in which they performed the services required of them, fully wrrrants me in saying that when more important and dangerous duties are assigned to them, they will willingly and cheerfully discharge them. Special commendation is due Colonel McClennan and his regiment for their splendid conduct on the 8th inst. The regiment was on that day for the first time under fire. Captain Andress, who fell mortally wounded, was a brave and accomplished soldier. His loss is deeply regretted by all who knew him.

Surgeon C. P. Harrington, Chief Surgeon of the Brigade, also Lieuts. Hathaway, Black and Yarger, members of my staff, each cheerfully performed his duty, and all proved themselves competent and skillful officers.

I beg most respectfully to represent that the eight days' rations required to be carried upon the persons of the soldiers, prevented rapid movements essential to the accomplishment of important ends in engaging or pursuing the enemy.

I am, Lieutenant, very respect'ly, your obd't and humble servant,
J. WARREN KEIFER,
Colonel Commanding.

Lieut. JAS. JOHNSON,
A. A. A. G., 3d Div. 3d Corps, A. O. P.

Battle of Orange Grove.

HEADQUARTERS 2D BRIGADE, 3D DIVISION, 3D A. C.
CAMP AT BRANDY STATION, VA.,
December 3d, 1863.

LIEUTENANT—*Sir:* I have the honor to report the movements and operations of my command from November 26th, 1863, to this date, as required by circular order of this date from Division Headquarters.

The command marched from Brandy Station at 8 A. M. November 26th, and arrived at Jacob's Ford, on the Rapidan River, at 2 P. M.

Before starting from Brandy Station, two hundred men were detailed from the 110th Ohio Infantry, under command of Major O. H. Binkley, as corps train guard.

About 4 P. M., the troops crossed the Ford and marched about three miles on a road leading to the turnpike road from Orange Court House to Fredericksburg. The troops were then countermarched to within 1½ miles of the Ford, where they bivouaced for the night. My brigade marched in the rear of the 3d Brigade, which was the advance of the Division on that day.

The march was resumed at 7 A. M., November 27th, and toward the turnpike road above named. On this day, the 1st Brigade was in the advance of the Division, and the 2d Brigade marched in its rear.

Brisk firing commenced in the advance about 12 M., between the enemy and the 2d Division of the 3d Corps. After some delay, my brigade was ordered by Brigadier-General Carr into the woods, with directions to form upon the left of the 1st Brigade, commanded by Brigadier-General Morris. On account of the density of the undergrowth in the woods, and the absence of roads, it was with some difficulty that I succeeded in reaching the position designated. Upon arriving in the vicinity of the enemy's fire, I discovered they occupied a hill to my front, upon the slope of which were posted the troops of General Morris's brigade. I determined at once to carry the hill and occupy it, deeming it the only defensible position that could then be taken. As I was marching my troops by the left flank, and along the hollow behind the hill, I ordered the two advance regiments, (110th and 122d Ohio,) as soon as they had become unmasked upon General Morris's left, to move by the right flank in line of battle, carry the crest of the hill, and take post behind a fence upon its summit.

The 6th Maryland and 138th Pennsylvania Infantry Regiments were ordered to file in rear of the two Ohio regiments and take position upon their left, from right to left, in the order named. The hill was carried and the fence gained with but slight loss. On account of misunderstanding an order, the 122d and 110th Ohio Regiments momentarily fell back a short distance; but upon being ordered back, retook their position, and became immediately engaged with a heavy force of the enemy.

The right of the brigade was found to be in advance of the 1st Brigade, leaving it in great danger of being turned by the enemy. I promptly reported this fact to General Morris, and urged him to advance his line and also occupy the crest of the hill, which he did after a slight delay.

The Ohio regiments maintained their position until near dark, when their ammunition becoming exhausted, they were relieved.

The 6th Maryland was under a heavy fire from the commencement of the action until near its close, and maintained its ground gallantly.

Two assaults were made upon my line, the first in front of the 6th Maryland, and the second in front of the 138th Pennsylvania. The enemy was formed in columns of attack not less than three regiments deep.— He was both times repulsed with very heavy loss. During these assaults Colonels John W. Horn, of the 6th Maryland, and M. R. McClennan, of the 138th Pennsylvania Infantry Regiments, distinguished themselves by their superior courage and gallantry. The 6th Maryland remained in its position until the battle was about ended. It was relieved about 6 P. M. Its supply of ammunition was also exhausted. The 138th Pennsylvania was withdrawn at night, and after the close of the engagement.

The brigade bivouaced for the night a short distance to the rear of the battle-ground. The men were supplied with ammunition immediately upon their withdrawal.

The enemy's loss in my front was very heavy. His killed and wounded were left upon the field.

During the engagement, with rare exceptions, the officers and men behaved gallantly, and deserve high commendation.

I take pleasure in mentioning the uniform good conduct of Colonel Wm. H. Ball, 122d Ohio, Lieutenant-Colonel W. N. Foster, 110th Ohio, Colonel J. W. Horn, 6th Maryland, and Colonel M. R. McClennan, 138th Pennsylvania Infantry, Regimental Commanders. They remained at their posts, and with skill and bravery urged on their men. Lieutenant-Colonel M. M. Granger, Major J. C. Hill, Captains Sells, Ross, Cornyn, Guss, Walters, Stewart, Prentiss, Bradshaw, Martin, Beaver, Rouzer, Spangler, Moore, McElwain, and many others, deserve high commendation. Colonel McClennan was severely wounded in the foot, late in the action, and was obliged to leave the field. Lieutenant James A. Fox, 110th Ohio Infantry, was killed. He commanded a company, and, as upon former occasions, distinguished himself. He rose from the ranks to his position in the army. He was not only brave, but an accomplished gentleman and soldier. He commanded the esteem of all who knew him. His loss will be deeply deplored by his many friends. The total killed in my brigade was one officer and thirty-two enlisted men; wounded, seven officers, and one hundred and thirty-seven enlisted men. A list of the casualties by regiments is hereto appended.

On the morning of the 28th, the enemy having retreated, the brigade was marched to a point between the plank and turnpike roads leading from Fredericksburg to Orange Court House. A short halt was made near Robertson's Tavern. The troops were put in position facing the enemy, where he was strongly posted behind Mine Run, between us and Orange Court House, and covering the two roads named. The troops bivouaced in their position until about 2 P. M., November 29th, when my brigade, under the direction of Brigadier-General Carr, was formed for an attack in line of battle, and in the rear of the 3d Brigade, 3d Division, 3d A. C., (Colonel Smith.) The attack was not made.

At 4 A. M. November 30th, was marched to the left upon the plank road and again formed, as before, for an attack, which was again abandoned. About 2 P. M. the brigade, with the other troops of the division, was marched to its late position near the center of the whole line.

The troops bivouaced in this position until 7 P. M., December 1st, 1863, when orders were received from Brigadier-General Carr to march in the advance of the division. The troops marched to Rapidan River, and crossed at Culpepper Ford about 4 A. M., December 2d. The march was resumed about 12 M. toward Brandy Station. The troops bivouaced about sundown near Richardsville.

At 12 o'clock midnight the march was resumed for Brandy Station, at which place the brigade arrived about 6 A. M., December 3d, and went into camp, where it still remains.

During the march, temporary delays were occasioned by getting upon the wrong road, and also by artillery and teams stalling on bad roads.—This latter was particularly the case upon the march to Culpepper Ford, on the night of the 1st inst.

On the entire campaign, my orders were received from Brigadier-General Carr, Commanding Division.

I beg further to report that many sick were conveyed from Brandy Station in ambulances, to their great injury and the inconvenience of the troops. The ambulances being required for the conveyance of the wounded, many of these men, although unable to perform the day and night marches, had to be sent to their regiments.

The wounded received all possible care and attention at the hands of the medical officers.

Surgeon C. P. Harrington, Chief Surgeon of the Brigade, Assistant-Surgeons Richards, Bryant, Owen, Cady, Thornton and Foreman, were actively engaged in the care of the wounded. The last-named remained upon the field during the engagement of the 27th of November, and amidst the danger, rendered important service to the severely wounded.

In conclusion, I beg to acknowledge the important service rendered by Lieutenant Wm. A. Hathaway, A. A. A. Gen., Lieutenant Sam'l J. Yarger, Act. Asst. Inspector General, and Lieutenants Thos. S. Black and E. S. Narvell, A. A. D. C.'s on my staff. During the engagement they each displayed cool courage and excellent skill. For their prompt action in conveying orders upon the field, and skill exhibited in posting troops, I cannot too highly commend them. They also, upon the march, during the entire campaign, deserve commendation for their efficiency in the movements of troops.

I am, Lieutenant, with high esteem, your obd't and humble serv't.,

J. WARREN KEIFER,
Colonel Commanding.

LIEUT. J. JOHNSON,
A. A. A. Gen., 3d Div. 3d A. C., Army of Potomac.

Soon after the return of the army from the Mine Run campaign, the brigade went into winter quarters about two miles south of Brandy Station, on the east side of the railroad, and on the plantation owned by John Minor Botts. The quarters occupied had been constructed, in the main, by the rebels prior to the 8th of November, 1863.

The troops were bountifully supplied with stores and provisions during the winter, but suffered great hardships while performing picket and guard duty on account of the severity of the weather.

Orders from the War Department, promulgated through army head-quarters on the 24th of March, 1864, caused the 3d A. C. to be broken up. The 3d Division was assigned to the 6th Corps as the 3d Division of that corps. The 126th Ohio and 67th Pennsylvania, of the 3d Brigade, 3d Division, 6th A. C., were assigned to the 2d Brigade, 3d Division, 6th A. C.

The troops of the brigade and division broke up winter quarters and went into camp about the first of April, near Rixeyville, about two miles west of the Orange & Alexandria Railroad, at which place they remained until May 4th, A. D., 1864.

Battles of Wilderness, Spottsylvania and others.

HEADQUARTERS 2D BRIGADE, 3D DIVISION, 6TH A. C.,
CAMP NEAR CEDAR CREEK, VA.,
November 1st, 1864.

CAPTAIN: I have the honor to make the following report of operations of this command, commencing May 4th, 1864, and ending July 9th, 1864:

This brigade was composed, May 4th, 1864, of the 110th, 122d and 126th Ohio, 6th Maryland, and 138th Pennsylvania Infantry Regiments, and a detachment of men from the 67th Pennsylvania, temporarily attached to the 138th Pennsylvania.

The regiments were commanded respectively by myself, Colonel W. H. Ball, Lieutenant-Colonel A. W. Ebright, Colonel John W. Horn, and Colonel M. R. McClennan.

The brigade was commanded on that day by Colonel B. F. Smith, 126th Ohio. The brigade moved from its camp near Culpepper Court House, Va., at daylight on the 4th of May, and crossed the Rapidan River at Germania Ford about sunset of the same day, and bivouaced for the night on the bank of the river.

Early upon the morning of the 5th of May, Brigadier General T. Seymour assumed command of the brigade, relieving Colonel Smith.

EPOCH I.

The brigade moved, about 8 A. M., upon the Germania Ford Road leading to the Fredericksburg and Orange Court House Pike, but had not proceeded far until orders were received to return to and guard the ford and pontoon bridges, which it did.

At about 11 A. M., the brigade again marched toward the turnpike above named, and arriving near it, was halted upon a hill to the right of the road upon which it had marched.

About 1 P. M., orders were received for the brigade to proceed to the right of the line, and report to General H. G. Wright, commanding a division of the 6th Corps.

Heavy firing had already commenced along the line.

This brigade went into position in two lines, about 2 P. M., upon the extreme right of the army, the 110th Ohio and 6th Maryland in the front, and the 122d Ohio, 138th Pennsylvania, and 126th Ohio, in the rear line.

Under orders from Brigadier-General Seymour, skirmishers were advanced from the two regiments in the front line, who soon brought on a brisk skirmish. Captain Luther Brown, 110th Ohio, and Captain C. K. Prentiss, 6th Maryland, who were in command of our skirmishers, pressed the enemy's skirmishers back for a short distance, and closely engaged them, until about 5 P. M., when an advance of the brigade was made.

I received orders from General Seymour to assume general charge of the first line, to press the enemy, and, if possible, out-flank him upon his left. The troops charged forward in gallant style, pressing the enemy back by 6 P. M. about one half mile, when we came upon him upon the slope of a hill, entrenched behind logs which had been hurriedly thrown together. During the advance the troops were twice halted and a fire opened, killing and wounding a considerable number of the enemy.

The front line being upon the extreme right of the army, and the troops upon its left (said to have been commanded by Brigadier-General Neil) failing to move forward in conjunction with it, I deemed it prudent to halt without making an attack upon the enemy's line. After a short consultation with Colonel John W. Horn, I sent word to Brigadier-General Seymour that the advance line of the brigade was unsupported upon either flank, and that the enemy overlapped the right and left of the line, and was apparently in heavy force, rendering it impossible for the troops to attain success in a further attack.

This word was sent by Lieutenant Gump, of General Seymour's staff. I soon after received an order to attack at once.

Feeling sure that the word I sent had not been received, I delayed until a second order was received to attack. I accordingly made the attack without further delay.

The attack was made about 7 P. M. The troops were in a thick and dense wilderness. The line was advanced to within one hundred and fifty yards of the enemy's works, under a most terrible fire from the front and flanks. It was impossible to succeed; but the two regiments, notwithstanding, maintained their ground and kept up a rapid fire for nearly three hours, and then retired under orders, for a short distance only.

I was wounded about 8½ P. M., by a rifle ball passing through both bones of the left fore arm, but did not relinquish command until 9 P. M.

The troops were required to maintain this unequal contest under the belief that other troops were to attack the enemy upon his flank.

In this attack the 6th Maryland lost in killed two officers and sixteen men, and eight officers and one hundred and thirty-two men wounded; and the 110th Ohio lost one officer and thirteen men killed, and six (6) officers and ninety-three (93) men wounded, making an aggregate in the two regiments of two hundred and seventy-one.

Major William S. McElwain, 110th Ohio, who had won the commendations of all who knew him, for his skill, judgment and gallantry, was among the killed.

Lieutenant Myers, 6th Maryland, was also killed. Captain John M. Smith and Lieutenant Joseph McKnight, 110th Ohio, and Captain Adam B. Martin, 6th Maryland, were mortally wounded, and have since died.

Captain J. B. Van Eaton and Lieutenants H. H. Stevens and G. O. McMillen, 110th and Ohio, Major J. C. Hill, Captains A. Billingslea, J. T. Goldsborough, J. J. Bradshaw and J. R. Rouser, and Lieutenants J. A. Swarts, C. Damuth and D. J. Smith, 6th Maryland, were more or less severely wounded.

All displayed the greatest bravery, and deserve the thanks of the country.

Colonel John W. Horn, 6th Maryland, and Lieutenant-Colonel O. H. Binkley, 110th Ohio, deserve to be specially mentioned for their courage, skill and ability.

Captains Brown, 110th Ohio, and Prentiss, 6th Maryland, distinguished themselves in their successful management of skirmishers.

From reports of this night attack published in the Richmond papers, it is known that the rebel Brigadier-General J. M. Jones, (commanding the Stonewall Brigade,) and many others, were killed in the attack.

In consequence of my wound, I was not with the brigade after the battle of the Wilderness, during its memorable and bloody campaign, until August 26th, 1864, and I am unable to give its movements and operations from personal knowledge.

The brigade was commanded by Brigadier-General T. Seymour until his capture, May 6th, 1864, after which, with the exception of short intervals, it was commanded by Colonel B. F. Smith, 126th Ohio.   Colonel Smith is now absent from the brigade.

Early on the morning of the 6th of May, the brigade formed in two lines of battle and assaulted the enemy's works in its front, the 122d and 126th Ohio and 138th Pennsylvania in the front line, and the 110th Ohio and 6th Maryland in the rear line.   The brigade was still the extreme right of the army.   The assault was most vigorously made, but the enemy was found in too great numbers and too strongly fortified to be driven from his position.   After suffering very heavy loss, the troops were withdrawn to their original position, where slight fortifications were thrown up.   In the charge the troops behaved most gallantly.   The 122d and 126th Ohio and 138th Pennsylvania lost very heavily.

About 2 P. M., Brigadier-General Shaler's Brigade, of the 1st Division, 6th A. C., took position upon the right of this brigade, and became the extreme right of the army.

Skirmishing continued until about sunset, when the enemy turned the right of the army and made an attack upon its flank and rear, causing the troops to give way rapidly, and compelling them to fall back for some distance before they were reformed.   So rapid was the enemy's advance upon the flank and rear, that time was not given to change front to meet him, and some confusion occurred in the retreat.   Few prisoners were lost in the brigade.   The lines were soon re-established and the progress of the enemy stopped.   An attack was made by the enemy upon the re-established line about 8 P. M., but was handsomely repulsed.

Unfounded reports were circulated that the troops of this brigade were the first to give way, when the first attack of the enemy was made.

It is not improper to state here that no charges of bad conduct are made against the troops upon its right, but that this brigade remained at its post and successfully resisted a simultaneous attack from the front, until the troops upon its right were doubled back and were retreating in disorder through and along its lines.

About 7 A. M., of May 7th, the troops were moved a short distance to the left, and threw up temporary earthworks.   The enemy made a show of attack soon after, but were driven back and severely punished by artillery fire. Skirmishing continued throughout the day.

This brigade was detached during the Battle of the Wilderness from the other troops of the division, and received orders from Major-General Wright, commanding 1st Division, 6th Army Corps.

EPOCH II.

The march to Spottsylvania Court House commenced at 8 P. M., May 7th. The troops moved all night, and after a tedious and tiresome march arrived in position near Spottsylvania Court House about 6 P. M., May 8th, and found the enemy in front in strong works. Immediate preparations were made for an assault, which, however, was not made. After dark an advance was made as near the enemy's position as possible without bringing on an engagement. The troops were rationed for the first time on the campaign at this place. Breastworks were constructed along the front line.

The lamented Major-General John Sedgwick, Commanding the 6th Army Corps, was killed by a rifle shot in the head from a rebel sharpshooter, near the 6th Maryland Regiment, on the 9th of May.

On the 10th, a desperate attack was made by the enemy on the right of the brigade, which was handsomely repulsed. In addition to the continuous and heavy skirmishing, a furious artillery fire was kept up all day.

The brigade was moved from its position, on the 11th, a short distance to the left. Constant skirmishing still continued.

On the 12th, the brigade, with the division, was formed one mile to the left, about 11 A. M., in support of the 1st and 2d Divisions, 6th A. C., but was not heavily engaged. The 126th Ohio was detached about 12 M., and went to the assistance of Brigadier-General Wheaton's Brigade, 2d Division, 6th Corps. It was marched to the front line, and engaged the enemy. Fifty rounds of ammunition were exhausted before the regiment was withdrawn. Its loss was 16 enlisted men killed, and one officer and fifty-three (53) enlisted men wounded. Lieutenant-Colonel A. W. Ebright, commanding the regiment, was wounded in the head. He signally distinguished himself in this engagement.

The enemy was compelled to abandon his works in the night, and on the morning of the 13th was found in a new position, some distance to the rear.

At evening, the brigade moved back to the position occupied upon the 12th.

The morning of the 14th of May, the brigade moved to the heights on the north bank of the river Ny. The evening of the same day, the brigade charged in line of battle across the river, and took the heights upon the opposite bank, from which troops from the 1st Division 6th Corps, had been driven. The brigade at once intrenched and remained in position until the evening of the 17th, at which time it commenced to march back again to its position of the 12th.

The brigade reached its position about 6 A. M. of the 18th, and there remained under a heavy artillery fire from the enemy until 12 M., and then commenced a march again to its position on the south bank of the Ny River, near the Anderson House, arriving about 7 P. M.

The brigade moved forward on the 16th of May about two miles, but did not bring on a general engagement, and again entrenched.

Some changes were made in the line on the 21st, after which brisk skirmishing ensued.

EPOCH III.

The march from the position last mentioned to the North Anna River commenced at 10 P. M., May 21st, and was attended with no fighting, the brigade having been detailed as guard for ammunition and headquarters trains. On the evening of the 25th of May, the brigade was relieved from duty as train guard, and reported to Brigadier-General J. B. Ricketts, Commanding Division, and immediately went into position on the south bank of the North Anna River.

On the 26th of May, the 9th N. Y. Heavy Artillery, commanded by Lieutenant-Colonel W. H. Seward, joined this brigade. On the same day the brigade was marched about three miles to the Virginia Central Rail-Road, at Noel's Station, and immediately countermarched to its former position on the North Anna River.

EPOCH IV.

Leaving this last-named position, and re-crossing the North Anna River about 7 P. M., commenced the march for the Pamunky River. The brigade reached the river and crossed at Sailor's Ford at 12 M., on the 28th of May, marched about 2 miles from it, and again halted and entrenched. The brigade remained in position, skirmishing continually, until daylight of May 30th, when it moved with the division in a northwesterly direction, striking the Hanover Court House and Richmond Turnpike at the 17 mile post, about 10 A. M. Thence along that road to the Tolopotomy River, arriving upon its north bank at 5 P. M., where the brigade was formed in line of battle. In this position, the brigade remained until 12 M. of the 31st, when it was moved across the river and formed in line of battle on the south bank. Heavy skirmishing ensued throughout the remainder of the day, the enemy being in front in strong earthworks.— At 12 o'clock, midnight, commenced the march to Cold Harbor, (or Cool Arbor,) by the way of Salem Church, arriving about 10½ A. M., June 1st, 1864. The cavalry which preceded were relieved on the skirmish line by the 110th Ohio, Lieutenant-Colonel Binkley commanding. Entrenchments were hurriedly thrown up.

About 2 P. M., the brigade was moved from its works a short distance to the left, and formed in four lines of battle, preparatory to a charge, the 6th Maryland and 138th Pennsylvania in the 1st line, 9th N. Y. H. A. in the 2d and 3d lines, and 122d and 126th Ohio in the 4th line. At 6 P. M. a general assault was made upon the enemy in his works. This brigade carried the works in its front, and captured several hundred prisoners, who were taken to the rear. The captured works were held, and the enemy forced back. Repeated efforts were made by the enemy during the succeeding night to retake the works, but he was each time repulsed with heavy loss.

The officers and men of the brigade deserve great praise for their valor in this battle. I regret to say that I am unable to mention the officers who were most conspicuous. Colonels Horn and McClennan, who commanded the advance line, were particularly gallant in leading their men into the works.

The following communication was received, highly commending the troops for their conduct on that day:

"BY TELEGRAPH FROM HEADQUARTERS A. P.
Dated June 1st, 1864.

' To MAJOR-GENERAL WRIGHT: Please give my thanks to Brigadier-General Ricketts and his gallant command for the very handsome manner in which they have conducted themselves today. The success attained by them is of great importance. and if followed up. will materially advance our operations. Respectfully yours,

(Signed) GEO. G. MEADE,
Major-General, Commanding.

GENERAL: Major-General Wright directs me to say that he transmits the within to you with great pleasure. Your obd't serv't,
(Signed) R. F. HALSTEAD, Captain and A. A. Gen'l.
Brigadier-General Ricketts,
Headquarters 3d Div., 6th A. C.,
June 2d, 1864.

OFFICIAL:
ADAM E. KING, Captain and A. A. Gen'l."

June 2d the captured works were altered and strengthened for defensive operations. No general engagement occurred on this day, but skirmishing and artillery fire continued. On the 3d of June, Colonel John W. Horn assumed temporary command of the brigade, in consequence of the indisposition of Colonel Smith.

The brigade formed, 110th and 122d Ohio in the first line, 9th N. Y. Heavy Artillery in the 2d and 3d lines, and the 6th Maryland, 126th Ohio and 138th Pennsylvania in the 4th line, moved forward about 6 A. M., June 3d, a distance of two hundred yards, and then, under a heavy fire of the enemy, entrenched, using bayonets, tin cups and plates for this purpose. Many valiant officers were killed and wounded on this day.

From the 3d to the 10th, gradual approaches were made toward the enemy's works by means of zig-zag lines. Heavy firing was constantly kept up along the lines.

The 3d Division moved to the rear and left, about 2 A. M., June 11th, and halted in rear of the 2d Division, 2d Army Corps. At dusk, the division relieved the portion of the line then occupied by the 2d Division, 2d A. C. Colonel Smith resumed command of the brigade June 12th.

EPOCH V.

The brigade remained in the last-named position until 10½ P. M., June 12th, when it was withdrawn, and immediately commenced the march, with the division and corps, by the way of Hopkin's Mill. Moody's Farm and Emmitt's Church, to Jones' Bridge, across the Chickahominy River; thence by way of the Charles City Court House Road to James River, near Wilcox Landing, arriving June 14th. On the afternoon of the 15th the brigade with the corps formed lines and entrenched.

On the 16th, the troops were moved to the left and toward the river a short distance, and again entrenched. At 5 P. M., colored troops from the 9th Corps relieved the brigade, and with the division, it was marched to Wilcox Landing, and embarked on transports at 8 P. M. The main portion of the brigade disembarked at about 1 A. M., June 17th, at Point of Rocks. The 122d Ohio disembarked on the north bank of the Appomattox, at the confluence of that river with the James, marched, and joined the brigade at Bermuda Hundred, at 10 A. M. Nothing of importance transpired while at Bermuda Hundred.

The division was relieved at 3 P. M., June 19th, and marched and joined the corps in front of Petersburg at P. M. On the 21st, the corps moved to the extreme left of the army. The 6th Maryland and 110th Ohio, under command of Colonel Horn, relieved the cavalry, who were then engaged with the enemy. The brigade was formed in two lines of battle, and entrenched.

The 22d of June, about 7 A. M., an advance was made of one half mile, heavy skirmishing ensuing, in consequence of which the lines were halted and entrenched. At 2 P. M., the troops were withdrawn to the position last vacated. A charge was made by the division at 7 P. M., causing the enemy to give way precipitately. After advancing two miles, the troops halted and again entrenched.

Orders were received from Brigadier-General Ricketts, June 23d, at 6 P. M., to send three regiments to report to Brigadier-General Wheaton, Commanding 2d Division, 6th Army Corps. Accordingly, the 110th and and 122d Ohio and 6th Maryland Regiments were sent. The remainder of the brigade was withdrawn, and formed in rear of and as support for the 2d Division, 6th Army Corps. The brigade was withdrawn about 8½ P. M. to the position occupied on the evening of the 21st.

The works were strengthened on the 24th, and the troops were ordered to rest, for the first time on the campaign. Headquarters and regimental wagons were also ordered up to the troops, for the first time. The remainder of the 67th Pennsylvania, commanded by Colonel John F. Staunton, joined the brigade June the 28th.

The 29th, the brigade, with the corps, marched to Ream's Station, on the Weldon & Petersburg Railroad, and formed in position and entrenched. A detail of 600 men from the brigade aided in tearing up the railroad, on the 30th of June. At 6 P. M., the troops marched by the way of the Jerusalem Plank Road toward a point near the Williams House, and arrived the same night.

July the 2d, the brigade went into entrenchments at the Williams House, about 5 miles south of Petersburg. Colonel Staunton took command of the brigade on the morning of the 6th of July. Orders were received at 3 P. M., July 6th, to march to City Point embark for Baltimore, and from thence proceed to the vicinity of Harper's Ferry, Va.

*   *   *   *   *   *   *   *   *   *   *

Many officers who fell in this long and memorable campaign should be favorably mentioned, but the already great length of this report forbids my doing it.

I would do injustice to brave and valuable officers if I did not make mention of Colonels Wm. H. Ball, John W. Horn, Matthew R. McClennan, and Lieutenant-Colonels A. W. Ebright, Otho H. Binkley and Moses M. Granger. These officers endured the dangers and hardships of the entire campaign, and by their personal daring and good example, did much to secure the results attained.

It should not be forgotten that many of the *affairs* mentioned in this report as skirmishes rise to the dignity of battles, compared with many of the so-reported battles of this and former wars.

In justice to line officers, it should not be forgotten that they were the principal actors in managing the skirmishers, and were often for many hours, and even days, under the fire of the enemy's sharpshooters.

The men on the campaign, in addition to the many hard days' fighting, suffered uncomplainingly the severe marches in the heat of summer, and often without a proper supply of water, &c.

This long campaign, more than all others, illustrates the endurance, valor and patriotism of the true American Soldier.

EPOCH VI.

The division, in obedience to orders, took transports at City Point, July 6th, and proceeded to Baltimore, Md., where it arrived on the morning of the 8th of July. The 110th and 126th Ohio, 138th Pennsylvania, and the 1st and 2d Battalions 9th New York Heavy Artillery, and a detachment of the 122d Ohio, were immediately shipped to Monocacy, Md. The 6th Maryland, 67th Pennsylvania, and the remainder of the 122d Ohio, under the command of Colonel John F. Staunton, did not, in consequence of unnecessary delays caused by him, arrive at Monocacy, but joined the brigade after the battle of the 9th of July. The regiments that arrived at Monocacy, under command of Colonel M. R. McClennan, with other troops of the division, the whole under command of Brigadier-General J. B. Ricketts, took a most conspicuous part in the battle of Monocacy, and each lost heavily.

Heavy skirmishing commenced about 8 A. M., on the 9th of July. A general engagement ensued, which ended about 2 P. M. In consequence of the vastly superior numbers of the enemy, our troops were obliged to retire, but not until the rebels had been severely punished. The enemy's loss in killed and wounded was so great, that his future movements were materially delayed.

Captain Wm. A. Hathaway, 110th Ohio, was killed upon the field. He was an accomplished young officer, and had rendered his country great and good service. Lieutenant-Colonel E. P. Taft, 9th N. Y. Heavy Artillery, Captain G. W. Guss, 138th Pennsylvania, Captain Luther Brown and Lieutenant George O. McMillen, 110th Ohio, were among the dangerously wounded. Lieutenant-Colonel Taft has since had a leg amputated. Lieutenant McMillen has died. Many other officers were more or less severely wounded. Colonels McClennan and Seward, Lieutenant Colonels Binkley and Taft, Majors Aaron Spangler and Chas. Burgess, and Captains Brown, Snodgrass, Guss, Feight and others, were distinguished for gallantry in this as in many other actions.

* * * * * * * * * * *

For especial mention of the conduct of officers, and for full and complete details of operations of regiments, attention is invited to reports of regimental commanders, which are herewith transmitted. The reports of Colonels Ball, Horn, McClennan, and Lieutenant-Colonels Ebright and Binkley, are particularly interesting.

Lieutenant A. J. Harrison, 126th Ohio, A. A. A. Gen'l, Lieutenants John A. Gump and J. T. Rorer, (now Captain,) 138th Pennsylvania, Aids-de-Camp upon the brigade staff, deserve special mention for their bravery in conveying orders, and their good judgment in moving and posting troops. Lieutenant Harrison lost an arm and was captured at the battle of the Wilderness, after which the duties of A. A. A. Gen'l were performed by Lieutenant Gump. To Captain J. T. Rorer I am indebted for many of the facts contained in this report.

I herewith append a summary of casualties by regiments which occurred in this brigade from May 4th to July 9th, 1864, inclusive. The total loss during the campaign was two thousand and thirty-three (2,033) officers and men.

I am, Captain, truly, your obedient and humble servant,

J. WARREN KEIFER,
Colonel 110th Ohio Vols., Comd'g Brigade.
Captain ANDREW J. SMITH,
A. A. Adj't Gen'l, 3d Division, 6th A. C.

———

After the battle of Monocacy, the 3d Division marched to near Baltimore, but subsequently rejoined the other two divisions of the 6th Corps at Washington, and participated in the pursuit of General Early's army.

The brigade participated in skirmishes of some importance at Snicker's Gap, Charlestown, Halltown and Smithfield, Virginia, in August, 1864.

On the 3d of September, the army under Sheridan moved from Halltown to Clifton Farm, near Berryville, Va.

Battles of Opequon and Fisher's Hill.

HEADQUARTERS 2D BRIGADE, 3D DIVISION, 6TH A. C.,
CAMP AT HARRISONBURG, VA.,
September 27th, 1864.

CAPTAIN—*Sir:* As directed in orders, I have the honor to submit a report of the operations of this brigade at the late engagements at Opequon and Fisher's Hill:

OPEQUON.

This brigade was composed on the morning of the 19th inst. of the 6th Maryland, 138th and 67th Pennsylvania, 110th, 122d and 126th Ohio Infantry Regiments, and 1st and 2d Battalions 9th New York Heavy Artillery Regiment, commanded respectively by Colonel John W. Horn, Col. M. R. McClennan, 1st Lieutenant J. F. Young, Lieutenant-Colonel Otho H. Binkley, Colonel Wm. H. Ball, Lieutenant-Colonel Aaron W. Ebright, and Major Chas. Burgess, numbering in the aggregate about 2,000 muskets.

At 3 A. M. September 16th, 1864, the brigade marched from its late camp near Berryville to the Berryville Pike, and along the pike in the direction of Winchester, Va., crossing Opequon Creek near the pike, and about 5 miles from Winchester. Thence it was moved to within three miles of Winchester, and formed under the crest of a hill to the right of the pike and upon the right of the 3d Division, which was the right of the 6th Corps. Skirmishers were thrown forward from the front line, under command of Major Chas. M. Cornyn, 122d Ohio, who immediately became engaged with the enemy's skirmishers. This position was attained about 9 A. M. The 19th Army Corps was formed about 11 A. M. upon the right of the 6th Corps, its left connecting with the right of my brigade. Heavy skirmishing continued until about 12 M., when the whole line advanced.

I was ordered by Brigadier-General Ricketts to dress my brigade toward the turnpike and upon the 1st Brigade, 3d Division, 6th Corps. As soon as we commenced to advance, we were exposed to a heavy artillery fire from the enemy. The 19th Corps did not move and keep connection with my right, and the turnpike upon which the division was dressing bore to the left, causing a wide interval between the 6th and 19th Corps. As the lines advanced, the interval became greater. The enemy, discovering this fact, hurled a large body of men toward the interval, and threatened to take my right in flank. I at once caused the 138th and 67th Pennsylvania and 110th Ohio Regiments to break their connection with the right of my brigade, and move toward the advancing column of the enemy. These three regiments most gallantly met the enemy's overwhelming masses, and held them in check.

The 19th Corps soon came up, and encountered a very heavy force of the rebels in a woods to the right of the three regiments named. As soon as the 19th Corps engaged the enemy, the force in my front commenced slowly retiring. I pushed forward the three regiments until we came upon two batteries of artillery, (8 guns,) silencing them, and compelling the enemy to abandon them. The three regiments had arrived within less than 200 yards of the two batteries, when the 19th Corps, after a most gallant resistance, gave way. The enemy at once came upon my right flank in large force. Successful resistance was no longer possible. The three regiments had already suffered heavily, and were obliged to fall back in some disorder. The enemy regained a portion of the ground from which he had been driven. In falling back, we lost no prisoners.

The broken troops of my brigade were halted and reformed in a woods behind troops from the reserve, which had come forward to fill up the interval. As soon as reformed, they were moved forward again over the same ground they had traversed the first time. While moving this portion of my brigade forward, I received an order from Brigadier-General Ricketts, commanding division, to again unite my brigade near the center of the corps, and to the right of the turnpike, near a house. This order was obeyed at once, and my whole brigade was placed in one line, immediately confronting the enemy. The four regiments of my brigade, that were upon the left, kept connection with the 1st Brigade, 3d Division, and fought desperately, in the main driving the enemy. They also captured a considerable number of prisoners in their first advance.

Heavy firing was kept up along the whole line until about 4 P. M., when a general advance took place. The enemy gave way before the impetuosity of our troops, and were soon completely routed. This brigade pressed forward with the advance line to, and into, the streets of Winchester. The rout of the enemy was everywhere complete. Night came on, and the pursuit was stopped. The troops of my brigade encamped with the corps on the Strasburg and Front Royal Roads, south of Winchester.

This brigade lost in the Battle of Opequon, some valiant and superior officers. Lieutenant-Colonel A. W. Ebright, commanding 126th Ohio, was killed instantly early in the action. He was uniformly brave and skillful. He had fought in the many battles of the 6th Corps during the past summer's campaign. Captain Thomas J. Hyatt and Lieutenant Rufus Ricksecker, 126th Ohio, and Lieutenant Wm. H. Burns, 6th Maryland, also fell in this action. Each was conspicuous for gallantry on this and other fields upon which he had fought. Colonel John W. Horn, 6th Maryland, whom none excelled for distinguished bravery, was severely if not mortally wounded. Colonel Wm. H. Ball, 122d Ohio, received a wound from a shell, but did not quit the field. He maintained his usual reputation for cool courage and excellent judgment and skill. Captain John S. Stucky, 138th Pennsylvania, lost a leg. Major Chas. M. Cornyn, 122d Ohio, Captains Feight and Walter, 138th Pennsylvania, Captain Williams, Lieutenants Patterson, Wells and Crooks, 126th Ohio, Captains Hawkins and Rouzer and Lieutenant Smith, 6th Maryland, Lieutenants Fish and Calvin, 9th N. Y. Heavy Artillery, Captains Van Eaton and Trimble and Lieutenants Deeter and Simes, 110th Ohio, are among the many officers more or less severely wounded. (Lieutenant Deeter, 110th Ohio, has since died.) I cannot too highly commend their gallantry.

Captain J. P. Dudrow, 122d Ohio, and Lieutenant R. W. Wiley, were each slightly wounded while acting as A. D. C.'s upon my staff.

The aggregate loss in killed and wounded in the brigade was, 4 officers and 46 enlisted men killed, and 24 officers and 264 enlisted men wounded, making an aggregate loss in the brigade, at the Battle of Opequon, of 28 officers and 310 enlisted men.

The enemy was pursued on the 20th to Fisher's Hill, about $1\frac{1}{2}$ miles south of Strasburg, Va., on the Staunton Turnpike, where he was found strongly fortified in an apparently impregnable position.

This brigade bivouaced with the Corps near Strasburg, Va.

FISHER'S HILL.

About 12 M. on the 21st, the brigade, except the 9th N. Y. Heavy Artillery, which was detailed as wagon guard, moved with the corps to the right of Strasburg, and was formed again upon the extreme right of the corps.

In compliance with an order from Brigadier-General Ricketts, I ordered forward the 126th Ohio, commanded by Captain G. W. Hoge, to aid in driving the enemy from a hill in our front. The regiment became engaged with the enemy. The 6th Maryland, commanded by Captain C. K. Prentice, was soon after ordered forward to its support. After a brisk fight, the two regiments charged and took the heights, thereby gaining a very important position, upon which the troops bivouaced for the night. In this affair, the 126th Ohio had 4 enlisted men killed and 17 wounded, and the 6th Maryland had 7 enlisted men wounded. Captains Hoge and Prentice displayed great gallantry in this action.

The brigade remained in the position occupied on the night of the 21st inst. until about 12 M. of the 22d inst. The 6th Maryland, being on the skirmish line, was constantly engaged with the enemy's skirmishers.— At the hour last named, as directed by Brigadier-General Ricketts, the brigade moved off to the right and upon the enemy's left, and with the 1st Brigade, 3d Division, as a support, attacked and drove the enemy from two hills which they held in considerable force. So rapid was their flight, that they abandoned shelter tents, blankets, and a considerable amount of infantry ammunition. During this advance, I ordered the 6th Maryland to push forward upon the extreme left of my skirmish line, to resist an attack from the enemy in that direction, which it was successful in doing. In this attack, portions of the 110th and 122d Ohio were thrown forward as a strong line of skirmishers, under command of Lieutenant-Colonel M. M. Granger, 122d Ohio. Major Aaron Spangler commanded the 110th Ohio.* Colonel Granger and Major Spangler exhibited their usual skill and good judgment in the successful management of troops.

The skirmishers were pushed over the crest of the hill and to within long rifle range of the enemy's main works, in which were mounted heavy guns. The brigade was formed behind the crest of the hill, confronting the enemy. Although near the enemy, he was not able to do us much injury with his artillery.

Sharp skirmishing continued until about 4 P. M., when the 8th Corps commenced an advance some distance further to the right, and upon the

---

*Lieutenant-Colonel Otho H. Binkley was corps officer of the day on the 22d, and received his orders directly from General Wright.

left flank and rear of the enemy. A heavy fire had been opened upon his works by artillery to my rear and left. My skirmishers were pressed forward, with orders to halt near the enemy's works and open fire upon his gunners. The whole line soon after advanced and charged the works, capturing many prisoners and four (4) guns, and dispersing the rebel infantry in all directions. As we charged, a battery opened my men still further to our left. The 8th Corps came up on our immediate right and with them we moved forward without delay, and charged the last mentioned battery, capturing it also.

At about this time, the whole army commenced advancing. The 8th Corps and 3d Division, 6th Corps, being fully upon the enemy's flank and rear, pushed forward with wild and victorious shouts along the entire line of the enemy, from his left to extreme right, taking all his artillery in position, and capturing and dispersing his troops. Not a regiment or company of the enemy left the field in anything like order. Of the number of pieces of artillery captured, this brigade is entitled to the credit of eight, at least. The number of prisoners captured by the brigade, I cannot state. Many of them were left behind to be picked up by others in the rear. It is said that through neglect to place guards over captured artillery, other troops who came up later, guarded and claimed it as their prize.

The brigade pursued the enemy with the corps all night. The pursuit of the fugitive rebels was continued by the infantry to Harrisonburg, Va., at which place the army arrived on the 25th inst. Thus ended the glorious victory at Fisher's Hill, (the enemy's boasted "Haven of Security.")

The loss in my brigade on the 22d was very light, considering the result attained. Many acts of daring bravery were performed by officers and men of this command. Lieutenant R. W. Wiley, with privates O. A. Ashbrook, Co. "I," 126th Ohio, Wm. Wise and Elias Barr, Co. "I," 110th Ohio, rushed in advance of the line and captured Captain Ashby (brother of the late rebel Generpl Ashby) and 21 men. Sergeant Albert Routzan and private Elias Wreight, Co. "B," 138th Pennsylvania, were the first in a fort, in which they captured one officer and 30 men. Each party brought its prisoners away securely. Other instances of a similar character might be mentioned.

The loss in my command in killed and wounded, from the 19th to the 26th of September, 1864, inclusive, was 4 officers and 54 enlisted men killed, and 25 officers and 314 enlisted men wounded, making an aggregate of 397 killed and wounded. Hereto appended will be found a summary of casualties by regiments.

Throughout the two engagements, Lieutenant-Colonel Otho H. Binkley, Major Aaron Spangler, 110th Ohio, Colonel Wm. H. Ball, Lieutenant-Colonel M. M. Granger, and Major Chas. M. Cornyn, 122d Ohio, Captain G. W. Hoge, 126th Ohio, Captains C. K. Prentice and J. J. Bradshaw, 6th Maryland, and Major Chas. Burgess, 9th New York Heavy Attillery, and others, displayed great bravery, skill and energy in the discharge of their important duties. Colonel M. R. McClennan, 138th Pennsylvania, remained upon the field at Opequon gallantly doing his duty, until from exhaustion he was obliged to go to the rear. He was weak and still suffering from a recent illness. One or two officers only are known to deserve censure and punishment for their inefficiency and bad conduct.

1st Lieutenant John A. Gump, A. A. A. Gen'l., 1st Lieutenant J. T. Rorer, Brigade Inspector, Captain J. P. Dudrow, Lieutenant Chas. N. Kuhn, and Lieutenant R. W. Wiley, A. A. D. C.'s on my staff, were conspicuous for bravery and good conduct. Their promptness in the delivery of orders, and skill and good judgment in carrying them out, entitles them to the highest praise. The already great length of this report forbids my making special mention of acts of distinguished bravery by members of my staff. Captain Dudrow and Lieutenants Gump and Rorer had one, and Lieutenant Wiley two, horses shot under them while in the discharge of their duty.

Orderly Lewis Paul, 126th Ohio, was wounded and had his horse killed under him, while carrying the brigade flag in the Battle of Opequan.— Orderly Lewis Shreve, 6th Maryland, also had a horse shot under him.— Orderly Richard Netz, 126th Ohio, and those just named, were cool and gallant.

My orders were, throughout, received from Brigadier-General J. B. Ricketts, Commanding Division, and through members of his staff.

To General Ricketts and each member of his staff I beg to acknowledge my gratitude and obligations for their kind courtesy and uniform generous treatment.

Regimental Reports of operations, and a nominal list of casualties, are herewith transmitted.

I am, Captain, very truly your obedient and humble servant.

J. WARREN KEIFER,
Colonel 110th Ohio Inf., Comd'g Brigade.

Captain ANDREW J. SMITH,
A. A. A. Gen'l, 3d Division, 6th A. C.

General Sheridan moved his army down the valley to Strasburg, commencing the movement on the 6th of October, and arrived on the 8th.

On the 10th, the 6th Corps was detached and sent to near Front Royal, and on the 13th it started to march via Ashbey's Gap to Alexandria— destination, Petersburg. It was halted at night of that day at White Post; and about 2 A. M. of the 14th started by a forced march to rejoin Sheridan's Army, then at Cedar Creek, near Middletown. On the same day it took up the position occupied on the morning of the memorable 19th of October, 1864. The importance of recalling the 6th Corps was demonstrated on that day.

Battle of Cedar Creek, Va.

HEADQUARTERS 3D DIVISION, 6TH A. C.,
CAMP BEFORE PETERSBURG, VA.,
December 15th, A. D., 1864.

MAJOR—*Sir:* I have the honor to report, in compliance with orders, the movements and operations of the 3d Division, 6th Army Corps, at the Battle of Cedar Creek, Va., on the 19th of October, 1864:

The 3d Division, 6th Army Corps, occupied a position in two lines on the left of the other two divisions of the corps, connecting on its left with the right of the 19th Corps. The 19th Corps was in the center of the army; the 8th Corps, or Army of West Virginia, being upon the extreme left,—the whole army facing Cedar Creek. The troops of the division were to the right of the turnpike about one-half mile, and not to exceed one and one-half miles from Middletown. Marsh Run, which in places was difficult to cross, flowed through a ravine a very short distance in rear of the division, and divided the main body of the troops of the 19th from the 6th Corps.

The troops of this division consisted of two brigades, commanded previous to the 19th of October, 1864, 1st Brigade by Colonel Wm. Emerson, 151st New York Volunteers; 2d Brigade by myself; and the Division by Brigadier-General Jas. B. Ricketts. The 1st Brigade was located upon the right, and 2d Brigade upon the left, of the Division. The aggregate strength present for duty in line was one hundred and fifty-one (151) officers and thirty-eight hundred and eighteen (3818) enlisted men.

On the morning of October 19th, at early daybreak, some firing was heard upon the right of the army, and soon after, rapid firing in the direction of the extreme left of the army. Being in command of the 2d Brigade at that time, it was immediately placed under arms, tents struck, wagons packed, and preparations made for meeting any emergency.

Immediately after the troops were formed in front of their camps, Captain A. J. Smith, A. A. A. Gen'l 3d Division, with others of the division staff, reported to me with orders from General Ricketts to assume command of the division, General Ricketts having assumed command of the corps, General Wright being in command of the army. I at once turned over the command of the 2d Brigade to Colonel Wm. H. Ball, 122d Ohio, and assumed command of the division.

The firing continued to grow more rapid upon the left of the army, and it soon became apparent that the enemy designed to bring on a general engagement. I received an order from General Ricketts to move the division to the turnpike, and commenced the movement; but soon after received an order to re-occupy the late position and look out for the right, as the 1st and 2d Divisions of the corps had been ordered from the right across the stream to the turnpike, and to the support of the left of the army. The firing continued more rapid upon the left, and extended to the rear parallel with the turnpike and toward Middletown. The troops upon the left had fallen back from their position in disorder; and with small bodies of cavalry, army wagons, pack animals, &c., had crossed Marsh Run and were rushing through the lines of troops. It was only by the greatest exertions of officers that the lines could be preserved.

While moving the troops back to their late position, orders were received to take the hills opposite the rear of the camps of the division.— When this order was received the enemy had gained them, and a portion of my command had opened fire upon him. Colonel Ball was ordered to take the position with his brigade. The rear line of the 2d Brigade, faced by the rear rank, was ordered to charge the hills, and orders were given to the other troops of the division to follow in close support. The troops advanced in excellent order, notwithstanding a heavy fire from the enemy; but just after the advance had crossed the stream the troops of the 19th Corps broke in disorder and fell back along the stream, and in such numbers as to impede the further progress of the movement and temporarily throw the advance line into some confusion.

Fearing the danger of getting my command into disorder, and at the same time ascertaining that the rebels had turned the left of the army and were already advancing and threatening the rear, the troops were withdrawn from the charge and a rapid fire opened upon the enemy, which stopped his further progress in my front. So great were the numbers of broken troops of the other corps that for a time the lines had to be opened at intervals, in order to allow them to pass to the rear.

In consequence of the necessary movements of the morning, the divisions of the 6th Corps were separated and were obliged to fight independent of each other. The 3d Division having faced about, became the extreme right of the army.

A number of guns belonging to the 6th Corps were posted upon the hills on my left. These guns, under the command of Captains McKnight and Adams, and under the direction of Colonel Tompkins, Chief of Artillery of the 6th Corps, were admirably handled and rapidly fired, although under a close and heavy fire of musketry. After over one hundred artillery horses had been shot, the enemy succeeded in capturing a portion of the guns, having approached under cover of the smoke and fog from the left, which was unprotected. A charge was ordered and the guns were retaken, three of which were drawn off by hand. Others were left in consequence of being disabled, but were subsequently recaptured. The regiments principally engaged in this charge were the 10th Vermont, (of the 1st Brigade,) commanded by Colonel Wm. H. Henry, and the 6th Maryland, (of the 2d Brigade,) commanded by Captain C. K. Prentiss. Great gallantry was displayed in this charge by officers and men. The rebels were fought hand to hand and driven from the guns.

A position was taken upon the crest of a ridge facing the enemy, who by this time had thrown a force across Marsh Run near its mouth, and was advancing along Cedar Creek upon my right. The right of the 3d Division was extended to near Cedar Creek, and the left rested a short distance from Marsh Run. A heavy fire was kept up for a considerable period of time, and the enemy were twice driven back with heavy loss.— Orders were received from Major-General Wright in person to charge forward and drive the enemy. The movement was commenced, and in consequence of the disorder into which the enemy had previously been thrown, bid fair to be a success; but owing to the enemy's appearance in heavy force upon the left flank of the division, the charge was soon suspended and the troops withdrawn slowly to a new position. The battle raged with great fury, the line slowly retiring, in the main in good order, from one position to another. My line was at no time driven from any position, but was withdrawn from one position to another under orders and each time after the enemy had been repulsed in all attacks from the front.

About 10 A. M., the troops reached a road that ran parallel to my line and at right angles to the turnpike, and a short distance to the rear and right of Middletown. The troops had been withdrawn not to exceed one and one-half miles from the position occupied in the morning. At this hour the enemy suspended further attacks, but concentrated a heavy artillery fire upon the troops. In retiring, almost all the wounded of the division were brought off, and but few prisoners were lost.

From this position the division was moved under orders to the left, and formed connection with the 2d Division, 6th Army Corps. After General Ricketts* was wounded, Brigadier-General G. W. Getty assumed command of the corps, from whom I received orders. The 1st Division, commanded by Brigadier-General Frank Wheaton, was formed upon my right. Many of the troops thrown into disorder early in the engagement were reformed and brought into line. Those of the 19th Corps were formed upon the right of the army.

It was known about 10½ A. M., that Major-General Sheridan had arrived upon the field, and had assumed command of the army. Major-General Wright resumed command of the 6th Army Corps.

Unfortunately, Colonel Emerson, commanding the 1st Brigade, failed to keep connection with the 2d Brigade of the division during a march to the rear, in consequence of which some delay took place in getting into proper position. As soon as a position was taken up, a heavy line of skirmishers was ordered forward from the 2d Brigade, to cover the front of the division. Colonel Ball, commanding 2d Brigade, accordingly ordered forward the 110th Ohio and 138th Pennsylvania Volunteers, under command of Lieutenant-Colonel Otho H. Binkley. They took up a position about three hundred yards to the front, and along the outskirts of a wood. Desultory firing and skirmishing was kept up.

The enemy, about 1. P. M., attempted another advance, and after a brisk fight with the skirmishers, caused them to fall back to the main line.— The attack was then immediately repulsed, and the skirmishers retook their former position. A small detachment of the Army of West Virginia, under command of Colonel R. B. Hays, of the 23d Ohio, was formed upon the left of the 3d Division, and connected with the right of the 2d Division, 6th Army Corps, the left of which rested upon the valley turnpike, about one mile in rear of Middletown. The troops remained in position until 15 minutes past 3 P. M., when a general advance was made, the order to do so having been received by me from Major-General Wright. Immediately after the advance commenced, the troops of the Army of West Virginia were withdrawn from the line, leaving a short

---

*General Ricketts was wounded, about 7 A. M., through the right shoulder and chest, but has since partially recovered.

interval between the right of my line and that of General G. W. Getty, commanding 2d Division. In accordance with instructions of Major-General Wright, my line was ordered to dress to the left, in the general advance, and close up all intervals. Specific instructions were given by me to brigade commanders to dress their troops to the left in the advance, leave no intervals, and to be careful to avoid dressing them too rapidly and closely. The troops were in one line of battle, and without reserves. When the advance commenced, the division moved forward in gallant style and very rapidly. It soon encountered the enemy in great strength, and well posted. The enemy opened a deadly fire with artillery and musketry upon the troops; but for a time they continued the advance, although suffering heavy losses.

The order to avoid massing the troops in the advance was not complied with by the 1st Brigade, the troops of which, after coming under fire, dressed hastily and in some confusion to the left, and soon became massed behind and merged into troops of the 2d Brigade. In addition to the confusion that necessarily ensued, the right was left unprotected. The greater portion of the division, after returning the enemy's fire vigorously for a short time, temporarily gave way. To the failure to keep the troops properly dressed, and to the fact that the 3d Division moved forward too rapidly and in advance of the troops upon its right, I mainly attribute the failure to succeed in this first advance. The troops on my left also temporarily gave way. The division lost very heavily in this attack. Not to exceed five minutes elapsed before the troops had been halted and were again charging forward. The enemy this time gave way, and were forced back several hundred yards, where they again took up a position behind a stone fence upon the face of a hill sloping toward my troops. The division charged forward to a stone fence which was parallel to the enemy's position, and about two hundred and fifty yards distant therefrom. An open field lay between the opposing troops. A stone wall extended at right angles from the right of my line to the left of the enemy's. A sharp and fierce musketry fire was kept up between the contending forces for about three quarters of an hour.

Orders were received from Major-General Wright in person to charge the enemy's position. Preparatory to giving the order for the division to charge, I ordered Colonel Emerson to send a competent staff officer with volunteer soldiers along and under cover of the stone wall upon the right of the line, with directions to throw themselves upon the enemy's left and open an enfilading fire upon him. This order was immediately carried out, and had the desired effect. Captain H. W. Day, 151st New York Volunteers, and Brigade Inspector of the 1st Brigade, was charged with the execution of the order. His gallant conduct on that occasion was highly meritorious, and he deserves promotion for it.— Lieutenant-Colonel M. M. Granger, 122d Ohio, volunteered to assist in this strategic movement. As soon as troops could reach the flank of the enemy, the division poured a destructive fire upon the rebels, and at once charged across the open ground, driving them in utter rout from their position. A considerable number of prisoners were taken in this charge; also small arms, and two battle flags. Leander McClurg, 122d

Ohio, captured the battle flag of what he supposed to have been the 44th Rebel Virginia Regiment, which he was forced to give up to a staff officer, not since recognized by him. Corporal Daniel P. Reigler. 87th Pennsylvania, captured a battle flag from a color bearer of the enemy.

The enemy retreated precipitately, throwing away guns, accoutrements, &c., in his flight. He was closely pusured by the infantry to and across Cedar Creek. His columns were completely routed, disorganized and demoralized. Troops of this division were the first to plant colors upon the works along Cedar Creek which had been abandoned by the 8th and 19th Corps in the morning.

The cavalry of the army was hurled upon the broken and flying troops of the enemy after he had crossed Cedar Creek. Night came on, and the infantry gave up the pursuit. Some abandoned and disabled guns and caissons of the corps were retaken on the ground upon which they had been left in the morning. The cavalry in its pursuit of the enemy captured many of the substantial fruits of the great victory which had been so richly earned by the hard fighting of the *Infantry* Soldiers. The loss in killed and wounded of the cavalry, compared to that in the infantry, was light, which of itself proves upon whom the burden of the battle rested and was borne.

At dark the troops under orders went into their respective camps, from which they had been called up in the morning. Many officers and soldiers spent the night in ministering to their wounded and dying comrades. Instances were not a few where the miscreant enemy had stripped the persons of our wounded of clothing, and left them without covering upon the ground. The bodies of the dead were generally robbed of all clothing and effects. It may be said, however, that many of the bodies of the enemy's dead had been robbed and stripped by his own troops.— A rebel officer was killed, upon whose body was found clothing and other private effects of Captain E. M. Kuhl, 87th Pennsylvania, who was mortally wounded in the morning.

*   *   *   *   *   *   *   *   *   *   *

Considering the unfortunate circumstances under which the battle commenced in the morning, and its long and sanguinary character, too much praise cannot be given to officers and soldiers.

Colonel W. H. Ball, commanding 2d Brigade, showed superior judgment, coolness, skill and gallantry. Colonel Wm. H. Henry, 10th Vermont. Lieutenant-Colonels M. M. Granger, 122d, and Otho H. Binkley, 110th Ohio, Jas. W. Snyder, 9th New York Heavy Artillery, and Majors Wm. D. Ferguson, 184th New York, Charles Burgess, 9th N. Y. Heavy Artillery, Charles M. Cornyn, 122d Ohio, and Aaron Spangler, 110th Ohio, together with many others, were particularly efficient in the discharge of their duties.

It is impossible to mention names of the many who displayed acts of distinguished gallantry.

The 9th N. Y. Heavy Artillery and a battalion of the 184th N. Y. Volunteers, commanded respectively by Major (now Lieutenant-Colonel) Jas. W. Snyder and Major W. D. Ferguson, for their noble behavior, deserve to be specially mentioned. The former regiment had several hundred recruits and conscripts who had just entered the service. The battalion of the 184th N. Y. had never before been engaged.

It is painful to mention the bad conduct of Lieutenant-Colonel Charles G. Chandler, 10th Vermont, Major Geo. W. Voorhees, 126th Ohio, and Captain Gilbert H. Barger, 122d Ohio Volunteers. These officers shamefully deserted their comrades in arms, and went to the rear without authority or good cause. Captain Barger had just received a leave of absence. He abandoned his company while it was in actual combat with the enemy, and under his *leave of absence*, attempted to shield himself from shame and disgrace.

*　*　*　*　*　*　*　*　*　*　*

Staff officers of brigades were very efficient in the performance of their duties. Lieutenants John A. Gump, A. A. A. Gen., J. T. Rorer, (now Captain,) Brigade Inspector, R. W. Wiley, A. A. D. C., 2d Brigade, and Captains Charles H. Leonard, A. A. Gen., H. W. Day, Brigade Inspector 1st Brigade, are among the most conspicuous. Lieutenant Gump was mortally wounded, and has since died.

*　*　*　*　*　*　*　*　*　*　*

Captains Edward M. Ruhl, 87th Pennsylvania, L. D. Thompson, 10th Vermont, and Orson Howard, 9th N. Y. Heavy Artillery; also, Lieutenants W. B. Rose, 14th N. J., August Phillips, 184th N. Y., Orson B. Carpenter and John Oldswager, 9th N. Y. Heavy Artillery, and Thomas Kilburn, 122d Ohio, were killed while valiantly discharging their duties.

Captain Wesley Devenney, 110th Ohio, and others of the division, have since died of their wounds.

Lieutenant R. W. Wiley, A. A. D. C. on 2d Brigade Staff, was the only officer captured in the division. He, mistaking the location of troops, rode into the enemy's lines.

*　*　*　*　*　*　*　*　*　*　*

Of the good conduct of the division staff I cannot speak in too high terms. Captain Andrew J. Smith, A. A. A. Gen., throughout the whole action displayed great bravery, skill and judgment. Captain Osgood V. Tracy, Division Inspector, Captain George B. Damon, Judge Advocate of Division, and Captain Anson S. Wood, Chief of Pioneers, each carried orders faithfully and gallantly in the thickest of the battle. Each member of the division staff was especially efficient and active in preserving lines, keeping up and urging on the troops.

Captain George J. Oaks, Acting Ordnance Officer of Division, deserves much credit for his energy and efficiency in supplying the troops with ammunition.

Robert Barr, 67th Pennsylvania, Chief Surgeon of the Division, W. A. Childs, 10th Vermont, and Wm. M. Houston, 122d Ohio, Chief Surgeons of Brigades, with the other medical officers of the division, deserve high commendation for their great skill and energy in taking care of and ministering to the many wounded.

Forty-three officers and six hundred and thirty-two enlisted men were killed and wounded in the division.

A summary of casualties by divisions is hereto appended.

Copies of brigade and regimental reports are herewith transmitted.

I am, Major, with high esteem, your most obedient and humble servant,

J. WARREN KEIFER,
Colonel 110th Ohio Vols., Brevet Brig.-Gen.

Major C. A. WHITTIER, A. A. Gen., 6th A. C.

Brigadier-General T. Seymour relieved me of the command of the 3d Division, 6th Corps, October 29th, 1864, and I again assumed command of the 2d Brigade.

On the 7th of November, the Army of the Shenandoah moved and encamped near Kearnstown, Va., (Camp Russell,) my brigade occupying the extreme right of the infantry. Some forts and earthworks were constructed by the brigade. The enemy made a feint attack on the 13th.

My command constructed winter quarters, but evacuated them on the morning of the 3d of December, marched to and shipped from Stevenson's Depot by rail for Washington City. At Washington the brigade embarked on steamboats, sailed at 12 M. on the 4th for City Point, and arrived at that place at 12 M., on the 5th of December, being the advance of the corps. On the 7th, the brigade relieved a portion of the 5th Corps on the front line, and went into camp, its right resting upon the Weldon Railroad, extending to the left of it, so as to include Forts Wadsworth and Keene.

On the night of the 9th, the greater part of the brigade, with other troops, went upon an expedition to Hatcher's Run; but returned on the night of the 10th to its old camp, where it remained until Februray 9th, 1865, building winter quarters, drilling, and performing heavy guard and picket duty. The 138th Pennsylvania garrisoned Fort Dushane, on the rear line, from the time of its arrival with the Army of the Potomac until April 1st, 1865.

On the 9th of February, the brigade again moved, and relieved a portion of the 5th Corps near the Squirrel Level Road, and on that part of the line including Forts Fisher, Welch and Gregg. Here the brigade again constructed winter quarters. It also performed much garrison, guard, picket and fatigue duty. From this time forward, one-tenth of the command was kept in the trenches and forts, by day and night, and very heavy garrisons were kept in the fort, under arms, at night.   The camps and quarters were within easy musket range of the enemy's outer line of works, and in full view of his camps.

All possible pains were taken to fully drill and equip the command for the final struggle, which was believed to be at hand.

The pickets of the enemy in front of Fort Welch were as near to ours as one hundred yards.   Picket firing was seldom indulged in until after March 25th.   The men mingled together between the lines in procuring fuel.   A large number of deserters came into our lines as the time for active operations approached.   Notwithstanding the many changes, hardships, privations and sufferings required of officers and men, all were unusually cheerful and buoyant in spirits.   Murmuring there was some; but when the time for battle arrived, that, too, ceased.

Battle in front of Petersburg, March, 1865.

HEADQUARTERS 2D BRIGADE, 3D DIVISION, 6TH CORPS,
CAMP AT BURKEVILLE, VIRGINIA,
April 16th, A. D., 1865.

MAJOR: I have the honor to transmit the following report of the part taken by this brigade on the 25th of March, 1865, in the charge upon and capture of the enemy's entrenched picket line, near Forts Fisher and Welsh, in front of Petersburg, Virginia :

This brigade, save the 138th Pennsylvania Volunteers, occupied the line of works including Forts Fisher, Welsh and Gregg, and about three quarters of a mile from the enemy's fortifications.   The enemy's picket line was strongly entrenched, and manned by an unusually large number of men.

About 1 P. M., on the 25th ult., I received an order from Brigadier-General T. Seymour, commanding division, to send two regiments to support our picket line in an attack upon the picket line of the enemy. I accordingly directed the 110th Ohio and 122d Ohio Regiments, commanded respectively by Brevet Colonel O. H. Binkley and Lieutenant-Colonel C. M. Cornyn, to move outside the works for the purpose ordered. Colonel Binkley was ordered to take command of both regiments.   The pickets of our division were composed of troops from the 10th Vermont and 14th New Jersey Regiments of the 1st Brigade.   Lieutenant-Colonel Damon, 10th Vermont Volunteers, had been charged with the movement of the picket.   The attack was made, but the greater portion of the picket line failed to advance.   The two Ohio regiments moved forward; but being unsupported on either flank, they halted before reaching the enemy's line, and subsequently retired to our own entrenched line. Both regiments met with considerable loss.   Orders were then received by me to take charge of the troops in person, and make the desired capture.

I at once moved out the 67th Pennsylvania Regiment. one battalion 9th N. Y. Heavy Artillery, and portions of the 6th Maryland and 126th Ohio Regiments, and under a severe fire from the enemy, pushed them forward to our entrenched line, preparatory to making the charge. At 3 P. M., at a given signal, the troops charged, and without halting to fire, passed over the enemy's line, capturing over two hundred (200) prisoners. In the last charge, the pickets from the 10th Vermont moved forward in good style.

Colonel B. F. Smith, 126th Ohio, Brevet Colonel O. H. Binkley, 110th Ohio, Lieutenant Colonels C. M. Cornyn, 122d Ohio and James W. Snyder, 9th N. Y. Heavy Artillery, and Major C. K. Prentiss, 6th Maryland, led their men with great gallantry.

Brevet Lieutenant-Colonel Aaron Spangler, 110th Ohio Volunteers, received a severe wound in the leg while gallantly urging the men forward in the last charge. Lieutenant-Colonel Damon, 10th Vermont Volunteers. did his duty nobly. Captain Simon Dickerhoof, 138th Pennsylvania Volunteers, who was division officer of the day at that time, showed great coolness and gallantry.

Notwithstanding a heavy artillery fire from the enemy's guns concentrated upon the troops, the captured line was held. It subsequently proved to be of great benefit to the corps, by enabling troops to be formed behind it for an assault upon the enemy's works.

Copies of regimental reports are herewith transmitted.

A summary of casualties is hereto appended.

I am, Major, your obedient and humble servant,

J. WARREN KEIFER,
Brevet Brigadier-General, Comd'g.

Brevet Major O. V. TRACY,
    Act. Asst. Ad't Gen., 3d Division, 6th Corps.

Battle in front of Petersburg, Va., April 2d, 1865.

HEADQUARTERS 2D BRIGADE, 3D DIVISION, 6TH A. C.,
CAMP AT BURKEVILLE, VA.,
April 14th, A. D., 1865.

MAJOR: In compliance with orders, I have the honor to report the operations of this brigade on the 2d inst., in the assault upon the enemy's works and in the engagement in front of Petersburg, Va.:

Previous to the 2d inst., my command, with the exception of the 138th Pennsylvania, occupied the line of works from Fort Fisher to Fort Gregg, inclusive of the forts named; and also Fort Welch, which was about the center of the brigade. The 138th Pennsylvania occupied Fort Dushane, on the rear line, near the Weldon Railroad.

The brigade was formed for the assault to the front and left of Fort Welch, about 3 A. M., in three lines of battle, with the right resting at an almost impassable swamp and ravine, which separated it from the left of the 2d Division, 6th A. C. The 1st Brigade of the 3d Division was formed upon the left of my brigade. The brigade was formed just in rear of the old entrenched picket line of the enemy, which had been taken from him on the 25th ult.

Much difficulty was experienced in getting the troops formed, in consequence of the darkness and the deep swamp to be passed through, and also a severe and annoying fire from the enemy. A number of men were killed, and a number of officers and men were wounded, during the formation of the troops: notwithstanding which the troops preserved good order, and remained cool and steady.

The 110th and 122d Ohio and 6th Maryland Regiments were formed in the front line, from right to left in the order named. The 9th N. Y. Heavy Artillery constituted the 2d line, and the 122d Ohio, 138th and 67th Pennsylvania Regiments were formed in the rear line, from right to left, in the order named.

The signal to assault the enemy's works was given by direction of Major-General Wright, at precisely 4 A. M., by discharging a piece of artillery at Fort Fisher. Immediately after the signal was given, the troops in the front line moved forward upon the enemy's outer works, which were held by a strong line of pickets, and captured them; and without halting or discharging a piece, although receiving a heavy fire, the whole command moved upon the main works. Not even a temporary check transpired in passing through and over the double lines of abattis, ditch and strong earthworks. A hand to hand fight ensued within the main works, in which many gallant officers and men fell killed and wounded. The rebels in our front were soon killed, wounded, captured or dispersed. Although the enemy had a large amount of artillery in the works in our front, we suffered but little from it. The whole of his artillery in our front fell into our hands immediately upon our entering the works.

This brigade assaulted the enemy just to the left (the enemy's right) of a salient angle in his line of works. After gaining an entrance within the works, the enemy were still firing over them to our right and upon the 1st and 2d Divisions of the 6th A. C., but in a few moments were driven from their entire line of works in front of the corps. This brigade captured ten pieces of artillery immediately after entering the enemy's works, for which it received receipts; also, a large number of prisoners, three battle flags, and Major-General Heath's division headquarters flag.

The troops of the brigade were in some confusion after entering the works, but the main body was at once directed along the enemy's fortifications to the left, and upon a strong fort containing four pieces of artillery, which was soon captured. Although a number of troops of the division were hurried to this fort, yet when attacked by the enemy, they were, owing to their unorganized condition, driven back, and the fort was retaken and held by the rebels a very short time.

At this juncture, I directed Major Wm. Wood and Brevet Major S. B. Lamereaux, 9th N. Y. Heavy Artillery, to place in position a four gun battery captured from the enemy, which they were prompt in doing, and fired it with good effect.

A portion of the 122d Ohio and 138th Pennsylvania Regiments, after passing over the works, continued directly forward across the Boydton Plank Road to a camp of the enemy, some distance in the rear of the fortifications, where they captured a large number of prisoners. Some of the troops continued as far to the northward as the Southside Railroad, and destroyed the telegraph and tore up the rails on the Southside Road. Upon their return, Corporal John W. Mouk and private Daniel Wolford, Co. "F," 138th Pennsylvania Volunteers, became separated from the other troops. Two mounted men with pistols in their hands rode upon them and demanded their surrender, which was refused. The mounted men told them that other troops were coming upon them. The Corporal and private deliberately fired upon the mounted men, the Corporal killing one of them; the other escaped. The Corporal and his comrade, fearing that others of the enemy were near at hand, retreated to the main body of the troops. From the manner in which it is known that Lieutenant-General A. P. Hill was killed, there can be no doubt that Corporal Mouk killed him. One of General Hill's staff officers, who was near him when he was shot, locates the place of his death where the Corporal related that he had shot an officer, before the death of General Hill was known to him.

As soon as the recaptured fort was again retaken by us, the main body of the troops of the brigade, with the other troops of the division, swept along the enemy's fortifications to the left as far as Hatcher's Run, and small parties of the brigade, with the brigade sharpshooters, crossed it and captured a large number of prisoners. Twelve pieces of artillery were captured during this movement to the left by the troops of the 3d Division. Captain Wm. L. Shaw, with a small party of men, captured a four gun battery and over fifty prisoners, near Hatcher's Run. The prisoners were brought away and the guns were turned over to Brevet Brigadier-General Harris's brigade, in the 24th Army Corps. As the prisoners were all hastened to the rear, I am unable to approximate to the number captured by this brigade.

From Hatcher's Run the troops were hastened back to the place where the attack was first made, whence the division was sent to the front, and formed fronting Petersburg, and upon the left and in support of the 9th Army Corps.

Particular mention has already been made, in a separate report, of the gallantry of officers; but it is due to Col. M. R. McClennan, 138th Penn., Lieut.-Cols. Charles M. Cornyn, 122d Ohio, and Jas. W. Snyder, 9th N. Y. Heavy Artillery, Majors Clifton K. Prentiss, 6th Maryland, Wm. and Anson Wood, and Brevet Major S. B. Lamereaux, 9th N. Y. Heavy Artillery, that their brilliant services should be acknowledged here. Major Prentiss, 6th Maryland, with a large portion of his regiment, was the first to penetrate the enemy's works, where, after a most bloody struggle, he fell severely if not mortally wounded.* Five other officers of the 6th

*Major Prentiss was wounded at the same time his brother, an officer in the rebel army, received a mortal wound. They fell side by side, and recognized each other. They were nursed and cared for in the same hospital. The former died in August, 1865, and the latter in June of the same year.

Maryland were wounded very soon after entering the fortifications. Too much praise cannot be given the officers and men of this regiment.

So nearly at the same time were the colors of the 110th Ohio, 9th N. Y. Heavy Artillery, 67th Pennsylvania and 6th Maryland, placed upon the enemy's works, that each claims the honor of being the first. Captain Wm. D. Shellenberger, 110th Ohio, received a severe wound in the arm while advancing upon the enemy's works. Captain H. H Stevens, 110th Ohio, was shot dead after entering the fortifications. Captains George H. Boyer, 110h Ohio, J. W. Moffat and C. E. Patterson, 126th Ohio, J. J, Bradshaw, 6th Maryland, and Charles Gibson, 122d Ohio, are among the many who especially distinguished themselves on that day.

Sergt. Francis H. McMillen, Co. C, and private Isaac James, Co. H, 110th Ohio, and private Milton Blickendefer, Co. E, 126th Ohio, each captured battle flags. Private George Loyd, Co. "A," 122d Ohio, captured Maj.-Gen. Heath's division headquarters flag. Sergeant Judah Taylor, Co. "A," 9th N. Y. Heavy Artillery, is reported by his regimental commander as having captured a battle flag, which he gave up to two officers, whose names are not known to him. The names of many other enlisted men might, in justice to them, be mentioned. They have already been named in a separate report.

Captain William L. Shaw, Acting Assistant Adjutant-General of this brigade, and other members of the brigade staff, deserve special mention for their good conduct.

Captain Harrison D. Yarmett, 122d Ohio Volunteers, who commanded the brigade sharpshooters, was particularly efficient and active. He showed superior skill and judgment.

My orders for the day's operations were received from and through Brigadier-General T. Seymour, who in person accompanied the troops in the assault. Major-General Wright and Brigadier-General Seymour were present with the troops, directing the operations of the day.

Copies of regimental reports are herewith transmitted.

A numerical list of casualties is hereto annexed.

I am, Major, your obedient and humble servant,

J. WARREN KEIFER,
Brevet Brigadier-General Volunteers.

Brevet Major O. V. TRACY,
A. A. A. Gen., 3d Division, 6th A. C.

Battle of Sailor's Creek and Surrender of General Lee's Army.

HEADQUARTERS 2D BRIGADE, 3D DIVISION, 6TH CORPS.
CAMP AT BURKEVILLE, VIRGINIA,
April 18th, A. D., 1865.

MAJOR: In obedience to orders, I have the honor to forward a report of the movements and operations of this brigade from the 3d to the 13th of April, 1865, inclusive:

After the movements and operations of the 2d inst., the brigade bivouaced for the night in front of Petersburg, Virginia. Early on the morning of the 3d, it was ascertained that Petersburg was evacuated on the night previous by the rebel army, and reports were received, which proved to be true, that Richmond, the rebel capital, was also evacuated on the same night.

About 9 A. M., on the 3d, this brigade, with the division and corps, commenced the pursuit of the enemy, by the Appomattox River Road, in the direction of Burkeville Junction, Virginia. The pursuit was continued on the 4th and 5th. Just after dark on the 5th inst., the brigade went into position on the left of the corps, in two lines, facing Amelia Court House, near Jettersville, Va., its left connecting with the 5th Army Corps. The front line threw up slight earthworks.

Early upon the morning of the 6th inst., the brigade, with the corps, advanced toward Amelia Court House, in the vicinity of which it was known that the rebel army of Northern Virginia had been concentrated. The troops moved forward about three miles, when information was obtained that the rebel army had withdrawn, and was then moving around the left flank of our army and in the direction of Burkeville Junction.— The troops were marched back by way of Jettersville, and moved upon a road which enabled the corps to strike the enemy's flank.

About 3 P. M., of the 6th inst., the corps came up with General Sheridan's cavalry, which was about one mile from a road upon which the enemy was moving. This brigade was in the advance of the corps. The brigade sharpshooters and 122d Ohio Regiment were rapidly deployed as skirmishers, and the other regiments formed in two lines in their rear.— Without delay, or scarcely a halt for the formation, the whole brigade was pushed forward, as directed by Major-General Wright, through Brigadier-General Seymour. During the movement, I caused two companies of the 110th Ohio to deploy to the right to protect that flank.

The enemy was moving troops and trains upon a road which extended parallel to our front. A short distance from the road upon which the enemy was marching, a brisk skirmish ensued between my advance and troops of the enemy; but the road was soon gained, and a considerable number of prisoners and wagons captured. The brigade struck the main road upon which the enemy was moving at the junction with it of a road which led off to the right, and at right angles with it.

The greater part of the skirmish line, 110th Ohio and 9th N. Y. Heavy Artillery, was ordered to pursue a body of the enemy which had retreated on that road. The enemy also had a section of artillery upon this road, from which they fired shell and canister shot, but without producing much damage. The troops in pursuit soon compelled the artillery to withdraw from its first position to a second. Although the troops had performed a march of over eighteen miles, they eagerly pressed forward, and were in the act of making a second charge upon the artillery, when orders were received, purporting to have come from Major-General Sheridan, to halt and allow the cavalry to charge. The cavalry charge was not made. The section of artillery was withdrawn, but it is believed that it was subsequently captured.

The 6th Maryland, 67th and 138th Pennsylvania Regiments were reformed in line across the main road upon which the enemy had been moving, and at once recommenced the pursuit. The rear guard of the enemy was soon overtaken and attacked. It was vigorously pressed for about one mile, to and across Sailor's Creek. The enemy being cut off from retreat by cavalry, under command of Major-General Custar, was forced to give battle, and for that purpose formed his line behind Sailor's Creek. The divisions of Generals Picketts, Custis Lee, and also the Marine Brigade, commanded by Commodore Tucker, the whole under the command of Lieutenant-General R. S. Ewell, are known to have participated in the battle. Artillery was brought within range of the enemy, and opened a destructive fire upon him. The 1st Brigade, 3d Division, and the 1st Division, 6th Corps, were soon upon the ground, and formed for an attack.

Although staff officers were sent to withdraw the part of this brigade that had been sent in pursuit of the enemy upon the other road, only a portion arrived in time to participate in the final engagement, in consequence of the refusal of officers in the 2d Corps, which had then come up on our right, to allow them to be withdrawn from their front. An attack was ordered to be made, by Major-General Wright, commanding corps, with the troops already upon the ground. A concentrated artillery fire was directed upon the enemy's center, under cover of which the troops advanced through and across the swamp, and at once charged up the steep hills upon which the enemy was posted. A severe conflict ensued as the lines of the opposing forces came together. A number of men were bayoneted on both sides. The enemy had a heavy column massed in rear of his center, with which he charged upon our troops.— Owing to the fact that our troops could only be fought in one line, the enemy succeeded in breaking through the center and gaining a momentary success. The troops on the right and left continued to advance, until the enemy's column in the centre was enveloped, cut to pieces, and captured. The enemy was soon routed at all points, and many general officers and many thousands of prisoners threw down their arms and surrendered.*

The rebel marine brigade fought with most extraordinary courage, but was finally cut off and captured. Commodore Tucker, Commodore Hunter, Captain Simmes, and about thirty-five naval officers, with the brigade, surrendered to me. It is impossible to give the number of prisoners captured by troops of this brigade. Two battle flags were taken from the enemy during the conflict. Corporal John Keough, 67th Pennsylvania, and Corporal Trustin Connell, 138th Pennsylvania Volunteers, each captured battle flags. Much gallantry and many acts of distinguished bravery were noticed during this day's attack. Unusual credit is due the troops for the vigorous manner in which they attacked the enemy, considering the long and tiresome march made on the same day.

Lieutenant-Colonel J. C. Hill, commanding 6th Maryland, was captured by the enemy, but soon after persuaded his captors, including a

*Lieutenant-General R. S. Ewell, Major-Generals Kershaw, Custis Lee and Pickett; also, Brigadier-Generals Barton, Corse and Lewis, were among the officers captured at Sailor's Creek.

number of officers and men, to surrender to him and come within our lines.

During the entire day's operations, Colonel M. R. McClennan, 138th Pennsylvania Volunteers, Brevet Colonel O. H. Binkley, 110th Ohio, Lieutenant-Colonels C. M. Cornyn, 122d Ohio, and James W. Snyder, 9th N. Y. Heavy Artillery, regimental commanders, showed great skill, judgment and bravery. Major William G. Williams, 126th Ohio, commanding 67th Pennsylvania, was particularly gallant. Major William Wood, 9th N. Y. Heavy Artillery 'while leading his battalion in a charge, received a dangerous wound from a canister shot in the face. Majors Anson Wood, S. B. Lamereaux, and Captains George W. Brinkerhoff, Henry J. Rhodes and Chauncey Fish, 9th N. Y. Heavy Artillery, and Captains George P. Boyer, 110th Ohio, Charles Gibson and Moses D. Wheeler, 122d Ohio, J. J. Bradshaw, J. G. Simpson and Charles Damuth, 6th Maryland Volunteers, and Simon Dickerhoof, 138th Pennsylvania Volunteers, are among the many who did their duty nobly. Captain Harrison D. Yarmett, 122d Ohio, commanding brigade sharpshooters, handled his men as skirmishers with great skill and success. Captain W. L. Shaw, 110th Ohio, A. A. A. G. of this brigade, Captains J. P. Dudrow, 122d Ohio, J. W. Jewhurst, 9th N. Y. Heavy Artillery, W. H. Abercrombie, 6th Maryland, and Lieutenant R. W. Cook, 138th Pennsylvania, Acting Aide-de-Camps, serving upon brigade staff, were particularly active, efficient and brave. Captain T. J. Hoskinson, Commissary of Subsistence of this brigade, was conspicuous for gallantry upon the field. Privates Richard Netz, 126th Ohio, and George Ickes, 138th Pennsylvania, mounted orderlies, accompanied me with the advance of the troops in the field attack, the former carrying the brigade flag. Their most commendable conduct should not be forgotten.

The troops were moved from the scene of the battle after dark toward Rice's Station, and bivouaced for the night about two and one half miles from the battle ground, and about three miles from Rice's Station. The remnant of the rebel army retreated, via Farmville, across the Appomattox River toward Appomattox Court House, Virginia, and was closely pursued. This brigade, with the division and corps, crossed the river at Farmville about 10 P. M. of the 7th, and bivouaced for the night.

The enemy was closely followed on the 8th and 9th of April until about 2 P. M. of the 9th inst., when the troops halted about six miles from Appomattox Court House; and were soon informed that General R. E. Lee had surrendered the Army of Northern Virginia. The rebel army was then in our immediate front, and not to exceed five miles from Appomattox Court House. The wildest enthusiasm prevailed among the troops upon being informed of the surrender.

Early on the morning of the 11th inst., the brigade, with the corps, commenced the march to this place, where it arrived on the 13th inst., and went into camp.

The 126th Ohio, Colonel B. F. Smith commanding, was detached from the brigade on the night of April 5th, to guard prisoners, and did not rejoin the brigade until April 15th, 1865.

Detailed reports of the operrtions of regiments are herewith transmitted. .

My orders were received from and through Brigadier-General T. Seymour, Commanding Division, to whom I beg here to tender my thanks for his u'ᵮ form courtesy to me.

The once defiant rebel army of Northern Virginia being utterly vanquished, the troops are in the highest possible spirits at the prospect of an early and general peace in our country.

I am, Major, with high esteem, your most obedient and humble servant.

J. WARREN KEIFER,
Brevet Brigadier-General. Comd'g.

Brevet Major O. V. Tracy,
    A. A. A. Gen., 3d Division, 6th A. C.

The brigade remained at Burkeville Junction until the morning of April 23d, 1865, when, with the 6th Corps, it commenced a forced march toward Danville, under orders, said to have emanated from General Halleck's headquarters, " to push through as rapidly as possible for the purpose of assisting in the capture of General J. E. Johnston's army." The corps arrived at Danville on the 27th, and halted, Generel Johnston's army having surrendered to General Sherman, on the 26th, at Greensborough, North Carolina.

The brigade remained at Danville until May 16th, at which time it moved by railroad to Richmond, Va., and on the 24th of May, was reviewed, with the corps, in Richmond, and at once commenced the march for Washington, D. C. The corps arrived at Ball's Cross Roads, four miles from Washington, on the Virginia side of the Potomac, the afternoon of the 3d of June, having marched through Hanover Court House, Fredericksburg, &c.

The corps camped at Ball's Cross Roads until its organization was broken up. It was reviewed June 8th, in the streets of Washington, by the President, General Grant, and others high in authority.

The brigade was mustered out by regiments, in the month of June, except the 9th N. Y. Heavy Artillery and 67th Pennsylvania Infantry.— The former was transferred to the defenses of Washington, but was mustered out in July following. The 67th, being a veteran regiment, was retained.

The troops of the 110th, 122d and 126th Ohio Infantry Regiments were mustered out June 25th, A. D., 1865, at Washington, and at once shipped by railroad transportation to Columbus, Ohio, where they were paid discharged, and each man sent to his respective home.

Farewell Order.

HEADQ'RS 2D BRIG., 3D DIV., 6TH CORPS, ARMY OF POTOMAC,
CAMP NEAR WASHINGTON, D. C.,
June 15th, A. D., 1865.

GENERAL ORDERS NO. 28.

OFFICERS AND SOLDIERS: This command will soon be broken up in its organization. It is sincerely hoped that each man may soon be permitted to return to his home, family and friends, to enjoy their blessings and that of a peaceful, free and happy people.

The great length of time I have had the honor to command you, has led to no ordinary attachment. The many hardships, trials and dangers we have shared together, and the distinguished services you have performed in camp, on the march, and upon the field of battle, have long since endeared me to you. I shall ever be proud to have been your commander, and will cherish a lasting recollection of both officers and men. Your efficient services and gallant conduct in behalf of *human rights* and *human freedom* will not be overlooked and forgotten by a grateful country.

I cannot repress the deepest feelings of sadness upon parting with you.

I mourn with you, and share in your sorrow, for the many brave comrades who have fallen in battle and have been stricken down with disease. Let us revere their memories and emulate their noble character and goodness. A proud and great nation will not neglect their afflicted families. The many disabled officers and soldiers will also be cared for by a grateful people and an affluent country.

You have a proud name as soldiers; and I trust that, at your homes, you will so conduct yourselves that you will be honored and respected as good citizens.

I shall part with you entertaining the sincerest feelings of affection and kindness for all, hoping that it may be my good fortune to meet and greet you in future as honored citizens and friends.

J. WARREN KEIFER.

Summary of Casualties by Regiments in the 2d Brigade, 3d Division, while serving in the 3d and 6th Army Corps.

	KILLED.		WOUNDED.		TOTAL.		
	Officers.	En. men.	Officers.	En. men.	Officers.	En. men.	Aggregate.
110th Ohio Infantry...........	10	102	18	443	28	545	573
122d Ohio Infantry	7	92	17	432	24	524	548
126th Ohio Infantry	9	111	10	379	19	490	509
6th Maryland Infantry........	7	103	21	213	28	316	344
138th Pennsylvania Infantry..	5	120	16	223	21	343	364
67th Pennsylvania Infantry...	2	90	3	130	5	220	224
9th N. Y. Heavy Artillery....	14	204	16	590	30	794	824
Total...............	54	812	101	2 410	155	3 232	3 387